NEEDLE FELT DOLLS

Dedication

For our mum who loved the sunshine, birds and flowers. We feel that this book was meant to be because in the sixteenth century the word 'doll' was derived from her name, Dorothy. She adored miniatures and had an amazing collection of all sorts which we happily inherited. We now use them as accessories and photography props for our dolls and animals in the many woolly stories that we love to tell.

Acknowledgements

Big thanks and woolly hugs go to the wonderful Search Press team, in particular Martin and Caroline de la Bédoyère for their support and belief in what we do, and Editorial Director Katie French who commissioned this book. Special thanks also go to our editor Lyndsey Dodd, photographers Mark Davison and Stacy Grant, and designer Juan Hayward. A big thank you to all our followers, readers and fans who continue to inspire and encourage us with their sense of fun and interest in our Woolly Felters' world.

NEEDLE FELTING
DOLLS
A COMPLETE COURSE IN SCULPTING FIGURES

Roz Dace & Judy Balchin

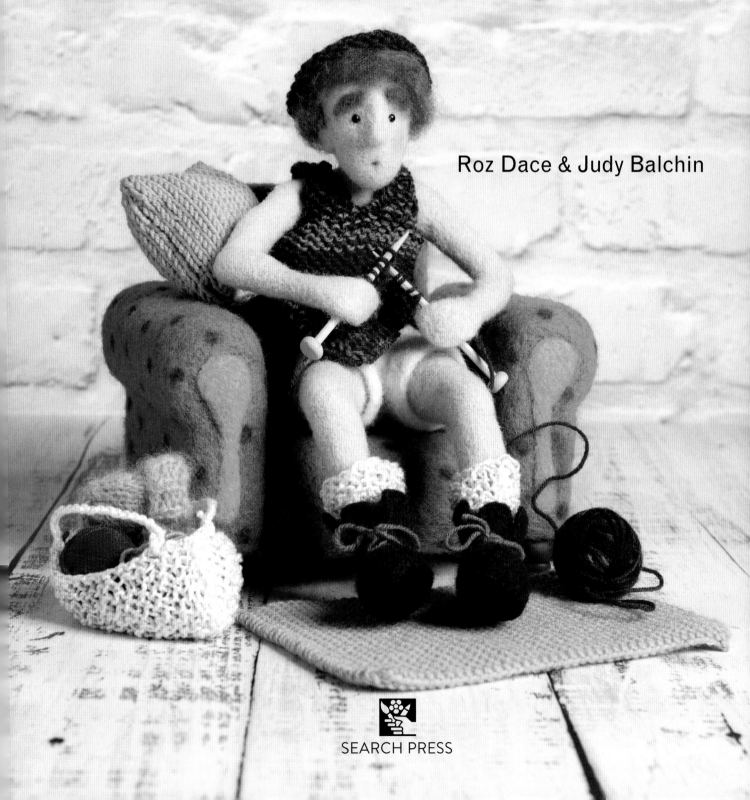

SEARCH PRESS

First published in 2023

Search Press Limited
Wellwood, North Farm Road,
Tunbridge Wells, Kent TN2 3DR

Text and templates copyright
© Roz Dace and Judy Balchin 2023

Author photograph by Rebecca Warwick
www.rebeccamayphotography.co.uk

Photographs on pages 1–6, 61, 62, 63, 67, 68, 69, 75, 76, 77, 83 (bottom), 84, 85, 97, 98, 99, 105, 106, 107, 117, 118, 119, 127 (bottom), 128, 129, 137, 138, 139, 153, 154, 155 and 161 by Stacy Grant

All other photographs by Mark Davison at Search Press studios

Photographs and design copyright
© Search Press Ltd. 2023

ISBN: 978-1-80092-013-2
ebook ISBN: 978-1-80093-003-2

Suppliers

If you have difficulty in obtaining any of the materials and equipment mentioned in this book, then please visit the Search Press website for details of suppliers:
www.searchpress.com

You are invited to visit the authors' website:
www.woollyfelters.com

Note on metric and imperial measurements

The projects in this book have been made using metric measurements, and the imperial equivalents provided have been calculated following standard conversion practices. The imperial measurements are rounded to the nearest $\frac{1}{16}$ for ease of use. For quantities less than 2g, we have said 'a small amount'. However, if you need more exact measurements, there are a number of excellent online converters that you can use. Always use either metric or imperial measurements, not a combination of both.

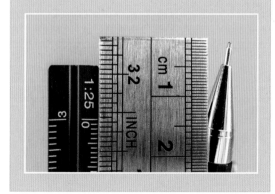

FSC
www.fsc.org

MIX
Paper | Supporting
responsible forestry
FSC® C012521

CONTENTS

Introduction

This book is a dream come true for us, combining our passion for wool and needle felting with our enduring love of dolls. It is an intoxicating mix that has inspired us to create a diverse family of characters ranging from a simple cone-shaped queen to a fully armatured Mother Earth. In our final project we invite you to step into a wonderfully weird world of 'Oddbods', where we show what can happen when you let your imagination fly. The projects are specially designed in sequence to build up skills with easy-to-follow instructions and top tips, and there is also a basic techniques section, all aiming to ease you into a wonderful world of doll making. Throughout the book we have included different characters, all offering tempting choices. Whether you are a fan of caricatures, storytelling, cuteness, realism or pure fantasy, this is the book for you!

One of the things we have discovered about needle felting is that although wool fibres can be manipulated and sculpted, they appear to have a life of their own. We have had many giggles along the way while working together in our Felty Towers studio, and even after our years of 'needling' we are constantly surprised at what can be achieved. The slight shift of a pose or a teeny tweak of the features can alter a look, while a change to hair colour and style can have a dramatic effect.

As you make your dolls we hope you experience the same joy and laughter as we do when they start to develop their quirky personalities. Do not be surprised if you find the technique to be strangely addictive and therapeutic. Our advice is to relax into this wonderful craft and enjoy your woolly journey.

Our love of dolls goes way back to our childhood when we shared a toy cupboard. This comfortable, jumbly corner was home to Sadie, who was literally loved to pieces, tatty Old Mary, and Peter – who is classed as antique now, with his painted china head and his curly wool body. Miniatures have always enthralled us too, with a passion that we inherited from our mum and Aunty Joan. We have gathered together a mini prop store that is stuffed with small things from weeny cups and saucers to doll-sized sofas and even cars. We use these accessories to tell stories with our woolly families and have included some here and there in the projects. They do add a little something extra to the characters, enhancing and enriching the stories that we and they tell.

Another delight for us is that we are following in the footsteps of an impressive and amazing doll history. The earliest archeological evidence indicates that dolls are possibly the most ancient toy known to us, with wooden dolls dating back to the twenty-first century BC having been discovered in Egyptian tombs. Throughout time dolls have been companions to children, collected and loved, used in magic rituals, or imbued with spiritual values. Voodoo dolls are among these mystical beings and they are strangely akin to the stabbing method of making that is employed by needle felters! During the early days of needle felting, folk artist Ayala Talpai brought this craft to the fibre art world's attention with her textile and doll making skills. Her aim was to keep things 'simple and affordable' using just one felting needle and few woollen fibres, and we thank her for her talent and vision.

Over the centuries all sorts of materials have been used to make these treasured companions and artefacts, including clay, bone, rags, china, soapstone, leather and much more. We are using only wool with its temptingly tactile and versatile qualities. So, as we leave you with our felting needles poised over an inviting, colourful array of fibres, we send our love to you and hope that you enjoy your doll-making adventure as much as we have enjoyed writing this book.

Happy needle felting!

About needle felting

Since we first took up the felting needle in 2013 we have loved everything about it, and we are not alone – there has been an international buzz as our wonderful community just keeps growing. What is so addictive about this stabbing technique? For us, the fact that you can turn a bundle of fibres into something amazing is just one of the astonishing things on our list of loves. Unlike wet felting the technique does not require water, which is why needle felting is also known as dry felting. There is very little sewing or gluing, materials are light, portable and they do not take up much space, and it does not cost much to get going. Also, many of us find the technique surprisingly therapeutic, perhaps due to the repetitive motion of the needle, or to the alchemic allure of wispy fibres shape-shifting into woolly wonders. As needle felting is not a quick craft it could be that the slowness allows us time for ourselves in a world that is full of pressures. Whatever the reasons, the satisfying 'crunch' of the needle as it moves in and out of the fibres has proven to be a soothing companion to many. If you are a newbie and wondering what all the fuss is about, have a stab at it and you may find that you will be joining us addicts in our woolly, joyful world.

In the beginning

Wet felting is thought to be one of the oldest crafts known to us, dating back thousands of years. Felt made with moisture and friction was used for insulation, protection, clothing and accessories for millennia. It was also loved for its ability to be transformed into colourful decorative art. Our craft is a young companion; but how cosy it makes us feel to know that needle felting is part of this ancient story. It stems from the mid-nineteenth century when enormous needlepunch machines were invented to produce felt products for industry. Each machine supported thousands of needles, all merrily jabbing away turning wool fibres into wadding (batting), insulation and other hardwearing products. In the 1980s, fibre artist Eleanor Stanwood acquired a small needlepunch machine from an abandoned wool mill in New England, USA. While she was experimenting, her inventor husband David wondered what would happen if he played with just one needle and soon he was poking and shaping loose wool fibres into solid shapes. Then Eleanor passed a handful of needles on to their friend, folk artist Ayala Talpai who delighted in letting her imagination fly with these 'tiny versatile things'. She eventually wrote her first workbook *The Felting Needle From Factory to Fantasy* in the hopes that it would inspire and attract others to experience the magic, which happily it did. Her second book, *The Felting Needle: Further Fantasies*, followed on, filling in the gaps and offering new projects and ideas.

How lucky we are that these innovative pioneers were so generous with their discovery and skill sharing. From these small beginnings there is now a fast-growing worldwide community of needle felters. We love being part of this global woolly clan as together we play, explore and enjoy a technique that offers so much to so many.

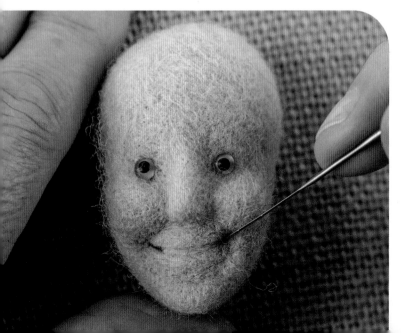

How it works

First there is the joy of wool. Versatile, tactile, durable and ecologically sustainable, it is at the heart of everything we do. Each fibre is covered with overlapping scales and these teeny 'hooks' are key to how the magic happens. Then there is the most useful tool in our kit, the felting needle, which has notches all along and around its shaft. This is when the poking fun begins. With each stab the notches catch on the scales, tangling the fibres into an interlocked mass. More poking results in a firm shape and this can be joined to other shapes to create larger forms. You will be pleased to hear that most mistakes can be repaired or adjusted with just this one needle, which is brilliant!

Simple shapes make up all the projects in this book and these are then sculpted, smoothed and embellished into the different characters, from small to big, and from realistic to oddbods. Once you are comfortable with the methods you will soon be on the way to creating your own woolly family.

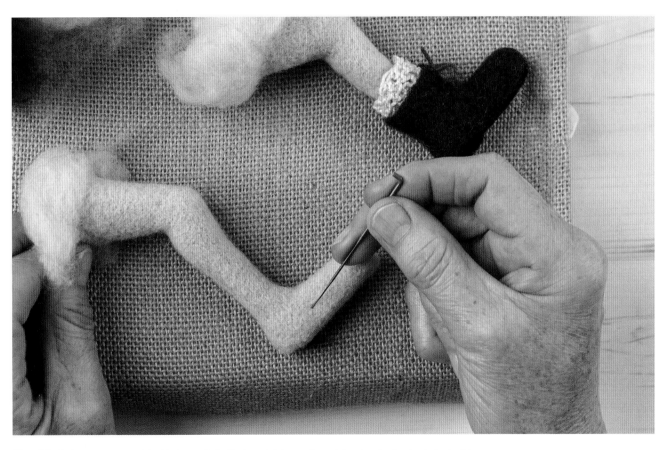

Simplified shapes are sculpted into realistic limbs which are then joined onto the body to build up a doll. There is no sewing, just the satisfying crunch of the felting needle as it binds the fibres.

What you need

One of the reasons why so many of us love needle felting is that with very few materials you can achieve so much. We started off with some wool, a couple of felting needles and a foam pad each and had great fun. If, like us, you go on to feel the magnetic pull of the magic, you can start adding to your basket of treasures. Here we talk about the tools and materials that we like to work with. You may want to explore others once you are happy with the technique, so our advice is to follow the journey through our book, get comfortable, then spread your wings and fly.

Wonderful wool

Wool has to be one of the best natural materials to work with. It is inexpensive, so beautifully versatile, and available in a wide range of weights and yummy colours. It can be purchased mainly from online specialist needle felting suppliers, but if you are new to this craft, choosing which wool to use can be more than a little confusing. Then there is the added frustration of different terms being applied depending on where you live. Do not panic! We give clear guidelines here to help identify what is what. Also, we have narrowed the choice down to what works well for us. Once you are comfortable with the craft, or you are already a seasoned stabber, you can have fun exploring other fibres.

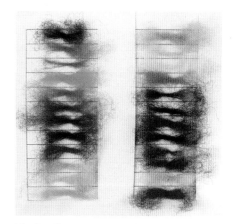

Most online stores provide inexpensive colour swatches that help you to choose just the right shade.

Which wool should you use?

There are over one thousand sheep breeds worldwide and the type of fleece depends on where the sheep live, so discovering the best wool for needle felting has been a fascinating and fun journey. In our early needle felting days we tried using raw wools straight from the sheep, but we spent hours picking out twigs and bits, and that was even before washing and attempting to dye them. If you are itching to start, you can buy your wool ready prepared and coloured as shown here.

Coarse wools have thicker fibres and we find that they are the best ones for needle felting. The thickness of each fibre is measured in microns and the higher the micron count, the coarser and thicker the wool. Our favourite count is normally between 30 and 36 microns. Other coarse wools have a slightly lower micron count, but there are no rules – our advice is to experiment with the different fibres. Generally we use a blend of Norwegian wools that we buy online, which are available in a wonderful range of colours.

Fine wools work well for adding small details, features and realistic-looking hair to our dolls. We normally choose superfine Merino with a count of around 18 microns. Because the fibres are so fine, they do not needle felt at all well. The stabbing process is frustratingly slow and the needle tends to leave visible holes, so the finish is not as smooth as it is with coarse wools. However these finer fibres are great for wet felting and we have used them to create clothing in three of the projects (see pages 114, 125–126 and 146–147). You can also use coarse wools in the wet felting process, but we only do this when we want to match colours to finish off a needle-felted garment.

Other fibres Curly Wensleydale locks, wiry Herdwick fibres and colourful silk sari threads are great for hair (see pages 83, 104 and 159). Glitter fibres will add a little sparkle, but they will not needle felt well on their own so we mix them in with the wool fibres before we start (see page 14). Silk fibres and wool nepps (tiny felted wool balls) give a lovely texture when used in wet felting (see page 147). Yarn is used to wrap the core wool tightly when creating an inner core for a needle-felted shape (see page 50).

Coarse wool.

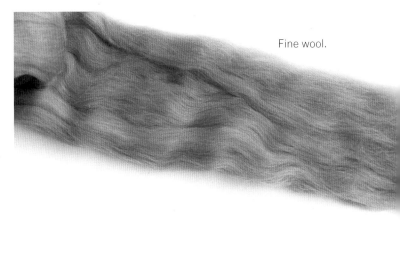

Fine wool.

Other fibres: Wensleydale and Herdwick wools, silk sari threads, glitter and silk fibres, wool nepps and yarn.

Wool terms

Batts and tops are available in a mouth-watering range of dyed and natural colours. All wools are available in different weights.

  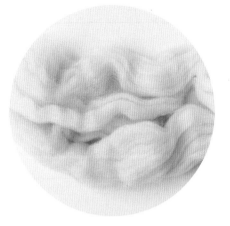

Batts are plump, springy sheets that are taken off a carding (combing) machine with their short fibres going in all different directions. The coarse wool batts are what most of us love and they are great for needle felting. Smaller or larger pieces can be easily pulled from the batt as you work.

Tops are also called rovings depending on where you live. These are long smooth fibres that are washed and carded into silky wool lengths, with the fibres all carded in the same direction. We use beautifully fine Merino tops for features, hair and wet felting. This is said to be one of the softest wools.

Core wool is cheaper than the other wools, it is available in natural colours and we use it to create a central core in our bigger dolls. We also wrap it around our wire armatures to build up the body shape before adding coloured wools. This speeds up the making process and it is an easy way to add bulk.

Storing wool

Wool should be stored away from dark and damp places. Beware of pesky wool pests who tend to lurk in cupboards and carpets. You do not want any of your precious wool stocks or sculptures ravaged by the larvae of insatiable clothes moths or carpet beetles. Fortunately we have not encountered the dreaded beetle, but what a nightmare we have had with moths. It was a few years into our partnership when we had a major 'moth attack' which wreaked devastation in our studio. We had to throw away badly infested wool, freeze retrievable wool to kill off the eggs and larvae, do a frantic deep clean and then totally re-think our storage options. We now know that these voracious insects can be managed if you follow simple guidelines. Store wool in sealed plastic bags or containers, in dry, light conditions. The wool eaters hate cedar and lavender, so liberally sprinkle your storage areas with these aromatic repellents.

Tip

We use aromatic cedar wood balls and lavender to repel moths and have sprinkled them all around the woolly places in drawers, containers and cupboards. It is worth getting some!

Blending colours

If you cannot find the colour you are looking for, it is easy enough to mix more subtle shades. When we are blending small amounts of wool we mix the fibres with our fingers, layering and criss-crossing them until we are happy. When blending larger amounts we use hand carders. These are an essential part of our studio equipment not only for creating new shades, but also for adding other fibres to the mix. We use them when blending Merino wools to create natural hair tones (see opposite). Glitter fibres can be carded with the wool to add sparkle to clothes and accessories. Drum carders are ideal for mixing and blending large quantities of wool.

A drum carder (below) and hand carders (below left).

Using hand carders

Carders cleverly comb and mix the wool. They have little hooked wires that catch on to the fibres and the more you comb, the more blended the colours will be. You can buy them in different sizes from felt making suppliers or specialist outlets online. Using the carders the right way is important. Follow the steps below with small amounts of wool. You do not want to lay too much on at a time. Reverse the instructions if you are left-handed.

Tip

There is nothing more frustrating than to run out of a colour halfway through a project, so always mix more wool than you need.

1 Lay the first colour on the left carder half way up the paddle, small pulls at a time. Layer the next two colours above the first row in the same way. Keep going until the paddle is full.

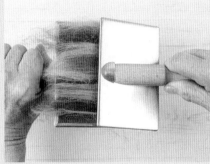

2 Place the right carder over the ends of the wool on the left carder with the handles opposite each other. Using a rocking motion, pull the handles apart. Repeat further down.

3 Repeat the rocking motion, moving the right carder up and down a few times. This will transfer the fibres from the right to the left carder.

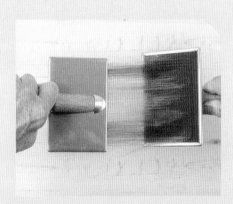

4 Now turn the carders over and continue combing and blending in the same way. This will transfer the fibres back from right to left.

5 When you are happy with the blend, remove fibres by placing the handles in same direction. Pull the carders apart.

6 Gently peel away the fibres.

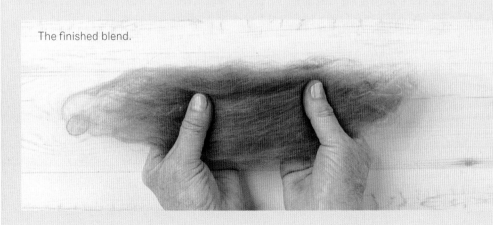

The finished blend.

Beautiful blends

Dive into your wool stash and get carding. Experiment and play with different colours as you join us on our doll-making journey.

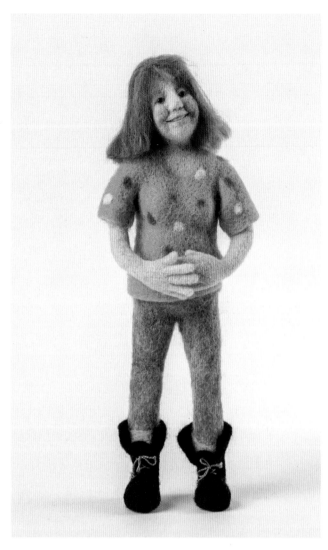

A Merino blend

We really enjoyed the challenge of making ourselves in the Perfect Portraits project (see page 128). This shows how to create fun selfies, and how to turn your family and friends into lookalike woollies! Here Judy's hair has been made with Merino wool using a subtle mix of browns and yellows which have been carded together into fine, smooth lowlights and highlights (see previous page). Her jeans have been needle felted with carded light and dark blue coarse wools to create a denim look (see the photograph of carders on page 12).

A glitter mix

Our Christmas Fairy is made more festive with a magic touch of sparkle (see the project on page 98). Glitter fibres and white coarse wool have been carded together to create a twinkle mix. These delicate sparkly fibres are then gently needled into place to create the skirt. Glitter fibres could also be added to her wings, and slippers in the same way.

Felting needles

About felting needles

The felting needle is our main tool. We can sculpt, blend, join shapes, add details, create character and expression, smooth surfaces, and correct mistakes with it. One needle can achieve amazing results, so it is no wonder that needle felting is such an attractive craft. We use just a small selection of different sizes for making the dolls in this book. Once you feel comfortable with the technique you may want to experiment with different needles.

Needle types

The metal felting needle has an 'L'-shaped handle with a notched blade (some call it 'barbed' although technically 'notched' is correct). The name given to each needle is determined by the shape and thickness of the blade. A triangle needle has a triangular blade with notches on three sides, a star has four notched sides and a twisted needle has a spiral notched blade. The thickness, or gauge, of the blade ranges from a thick 32 gauge to a very fine 42 gauge. Surprisingly the lower the number the thicker the blade, which initially gave us some woolly moments!

Needles can be bought either individually or in bulk from online specialist suppliers and from some craft stores. A few outlets will only categorize them as coarse, medium or fine but we feel that it is better to know exactly what you are getting. A general category may differ from store to store, depending on which supplier you go to.

We have had a lot of fun playing with all the different felting needles over time and are now comfortable with just a few 'must haves'. Our work is mainly small scale so we find our selection is ideal for what we do. The largest doll we have made is Mother Earth who is 34cm (13½in) tall (see page 139). If we worked on a bigger scale, then our needle choices would be different.

(see page 139)

Tip

The different needles look very similar so it is a good idea to colour code them. Dipping the handles in contrasting enamel paints works, and nail varnish does too.

- 40 triangle – red
- 38 triangle – blue
- 36 triangle – yellow
- 40 twisted – green

The needles we use

40 triangle

A great all-rounder. This needle is in the 'fine' category and we use it for everything from building up shapes to attaching body parts, contouring, adding features and detailing.

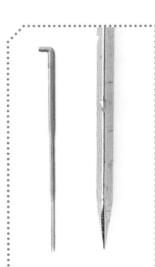

38 triangle

Although classed as 'fine' we find this needle is a good choice when working near partial wire armatures. It is thicker and therefore stronger than the 40 triangle needle.

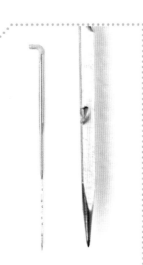

36 triangle

This thicker, stronger needle is the best choice when you are working near a full armature. We use it to secure wool fibres around the wire frame.

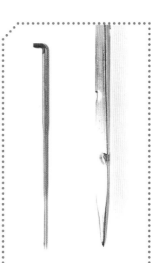

40 twisted

A brilliant needle for smoothing and finishing.

Looking after your needles

If you take care and follow our advice, felting needles can last for ages. They may dull over time, depending on how much you use them, in which case you will find that they do not tangle the fibres as they used to.

Be warned that if you do not use felting needles properly (see page 30), they will break and once broken they cannot be fixed. Although they are not expensive, breakages can mount up, so they could become the most costly part of your kit. Our advice is to purchase more than one needle when you first start needle felting. It is always good to have a few spare as there is nothing worse than breaking your one and only needle when the end of a project is in sight!

Usually a needle will break in two parts, the sharp blade and the thicker 'L'-shaped handle. The blade is incredibly sharp and must be disposed of extremely carefully and safely (we use a sharps bin). If a broken blade lands on your working surface or floor, a large magnet can be used to locate it. If it remains stuck in your felted shape, you could use the broken needle handle or a bradawl to poke it out. Tweezers are good for foraging, and if desperate a craft knife can be used to open the shape up. We never leave a blade in the wool as it may surface at some later point when someone picks up a doll to admire it. Ouch!

Do not throw the handle away. It is great for applying spots of glue, or we use it to lever out overworked wool fibres during the sculpting process.

Storing your needles

It is important to store your needles away when you are not working with them. Sweep and clean up after each working session to make sure no strays are lurking under the furniture or in shady corners! We store our felting needles in the clear plastic tubes that arrive with our needle orders; these can also be bought from specialist online needle felting suppliers or some craft stores. We also make needle-felted pin cushions (see below), which are ideal for safe stashing. Other storage solutions include ordinary plastic containers, polystyrene or foam blocks, or corrugated card – slip your needles into the grooves.

! Woolly warning

Once felting needles break they cannot be mended, so do take care when disposing of them and keep broken parts well away from inquisitive children and pets!

Tip

Always keep needles safely stored away when you are not using them.

Needle tools

Wooden, plastic or metal needle tools, also known as needle holders, house one or more needles. You do not always need a multi-needle holder, but we have found that they are great for speeding up the felting process, or for needling felt flat pieces when we make ears or clothes. The highest number of needles that we like working with is five at a time. These handy tools are available from online needle felting suppliers and from some craft stores. We fit our holders with 40 triangle needles. They are easily inserted, so you can change the provided needles to those of your own choice, or replace breakages with no fuss. Check the manufacturer's instructions first for needle changing advice.

Single-needle tool If you find holding a single needle difficult you may find it more comfortable to use a holder. This will sit nicely in your hand allowing a firmer grip, and it would be safer.

Three-needle tool This can be used with one, two or three needles. With three 40 triangle needles it is great for speeding up the felting process when starting a project. Once the basic shape has been established with the three-needle tool, we move to a single needle for more refining.

Five-needle tool This is a spring-loaded tool with a clear plastic safety guard around the needles to protect stray fingers, and you can lock it when it is not in use. The guard limits the stabbing depth, so we normally use it to work on a shape once the inner core has been felted, or to needle felt flat shapes such as ears, clothes and accessories.

Finger guards

Accidents can happen with stabbing needles, especially if you are new to needle felting and not keeping an eye on your fingers, so these protectors are a good idea. Usually made from leather, the guards keep fingers safe.

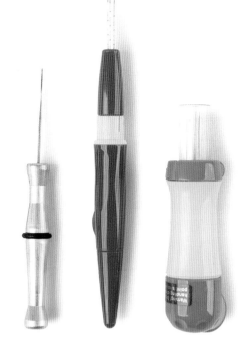

From left to right: single-needle tool, three-needle tool, five-needle tool.

Tip

Do not use a needle tool when you are stabbing near wire. It is far better to work carefully with one needle.

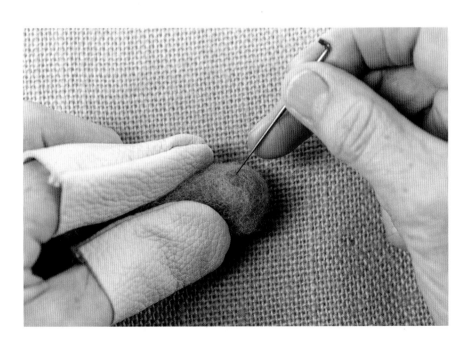

Needle felting pads

Felting needles will break if you work on a hard surface, which is why pads are an important part of your kit. During the stabbing process a pad provides a safe, protective working base. There are quite a few different ones available, but after exploring all options we always come back to the high density foam pads. We love working on them because they are firm and therefore absorb all the stabs. Foam pads are also called foam pillows, cushions or mats. They are not costly and you can buy different sizes from online specialist suppliers and some craft stores. When we started we bought some high density upholstery foam (a cushion pad) and cut it into 20cm (8in) squares, which is a good size for what we do. You may be eager to start, so a car cleaning sponge could be used, but this will start to disintegrate much quicker than a firmer pad, so we do not advise it. Finding bits of sponge in your work is not a good feeling! Even high density foam pads will start to disintegrate through use in time, so we prolong their life greatly by covering them with hessian (burlap). Eventually the hessian wears down, but it is easily replaced. If you are choosing this type of pad, it should be at least 4cm (1½in) thick so that the needle blade does not pierce through the bottom and break.

If you would prefer an ecologically friendly alternative, you could use a rice-filled pad. This can be bought through specialist online suppliers and some craft shops or you could make your own (see page 20). The great thing about this is that you can choose the size you want and it is totally recyclable. We use hessian to make ours, but you could use a different fabric. If you do, make sure the weave is loose enough for the notched needle to poke through, but tight enough to contain the grains of rice.

There are other eco-friendly woollen mats available which are durable and comfortable to work on, so it is worth exploring all options. Do look at what is available to find out which pad is best for you.

Tip

Protect your needles and always work on a pad when you are needle felting.

From left to right: hessian-covered pad, foam pad, rice pad, woollen pad.

Cleaning a foam pad

Small fibres will wriggle their way into a foam pad as you work and they will often cling to the surface. This can be frustrating because the tiny bits of wool can be transferred onto a new project, so it is worth cleaning your pad regularly. A rubber glove can be used to remove any unwanted fluff. Wet the glove and pull your hand firmly across the foam surface to dislodge the fibres, then allow the pad to dry naturally. Lint rollers or sticky tape can also be used. A final whizz over with a fluff remover tool will remove any remaining fibres. We use one side of the pad for light colours, and the other side for dark colours to avoid contamination.

Covering a foam pad

It is worth protecting your foam pad as it will start to disintegrate after a few months of enthusiastic stabbing. Hessian (burlap) is the perfect eco-friendly choice because it is durable, lightweight and comfortable to work on. You can buy it from craft outlets or garden centres, or you could recycle a potato or grain sack if you have one handy. Alternatively there is a tempting range of coloured hessian available online. Our intensely used covered pads usually last around six months before we have to replace them.

What you need

- Hessian (burlap), natural or dyed, 62 x 30cm (24½ x 11¾in)
- Dressmaking pins
- Sewing machine
- Matching sewing cotton
- Decorative ribbon, two 20cm (8in) lengths
- Foam pad, 27 x 24cm (10¾ x 9½in)
- Stamp and stamp pad

1 Fold the hessian in half. Pin and then sew a 1cm (½in) hem up each side.

2 Flatten the seams and then fold the top hem in 1cm (½in). Pin and then sew around the hem to create a hessian bag.

3 Pin one end of a 20cm (8in) length of ribbon to each side of the top of the bag and then sew over the ends a few times to secure.

4 Turn the bag to the right side. Fold the foam pad and insert it. Tie the ribbons.

5 To finish off you can decorate the hessian with a stamped design. Needles can be stored in the stamped area while you are working.

Tip

Covering a foam pad with hessian adds valuable protection, and prolongs its life.

Making an ecologically friendly rice pad

A completely biodegradable hessian bag filled with rice makes a great needle felting pad. It is easy to clean and will last a long time.

What you need

- Hessian (burlap), two 24 x 20cm (9½ x 8in) pieces
- Dressmaking pins
- Sewing machine
- Matching sewing cotton
- 280g (10oz) uncooked rice (any)
- Stamp and stamp pad
- Sewing needle

1 Place the hessian pieces together and pin.

2 Sew around three and a half sides approximately 1.5cm (¾in) from the edge. Repeat to strengthen the bag.

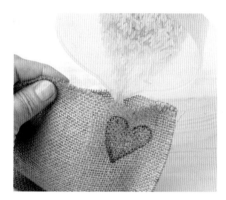

3 Decorate the hessian with a stamp and, when dry, pour in the rice.

4 Pin and sew the remaining edge.

Wire

If you use wire to create armatures for your dolls it makes them poseable and moveable, which we love. When we first started using it we bought thick jewellery wire. However, this proved to be a little expensive over time, so after experimenting we discovered cloth covered wire. This provided a good gripping base for the wool, but it was also expensive. Chenille sticks were great for small projects, but too weak for larger armatures. More experimenting went on, then by chance we bought a few rolls of galvanized wire from a garden centre. Now we use this inexpensive alternative for armatures and then thin jewellery wire for wrapping the thicker wires together.

If you are going to be making any of the armatures you will also need a good pair of wire cutters to cut and trim wire and a pair of round-nosed pliers to bend the wire.

Which wire?

Different thicknesses are needed depending on what they are used for:
- Thicker 1.6mm (16 gauge) wire is used to build the main armature for a larger, standing figure. We also use this thickness for necks and legs when we create partial armatures.
- Slightly thinner wires, 1mm (18 gauge) or 1.25mm (18 gauge), are good for arms on a partial armature. The thicker wire is used for larger dolls and when the arms have to be strong enough to support an accessory.
- We use 0.7mm (22 gauge) wire for the Christmas Fairy wings (see page 104).
- We use 0.4mm (27 gauge) thin wire to wrap, secure and strengthen the thicker armature wires (see below).

Tip

A wire armature gives flexibility and movement to a doll, which is great when it comes to posing your character. (See pages 52–53 for more on armatures.)

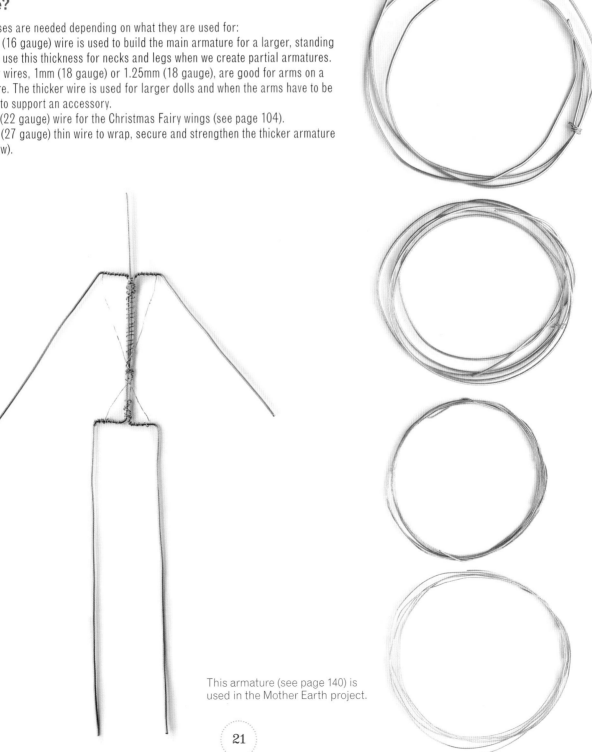

This armature (see page 140) is used in the Mother Earth project.

Other essential things

This is a checklist for the extra materials that we have used to create our dolls. You may find that you already have some of these in your crafty cupboards.

Pincushion for all your needles and pins.

Sewing needles, cotton for jointing, sewing clothing and lacing boots.

Yarn used to wrap core wool, make boot laces, knit clothes and accessories.

Fuzz remover used to remove flyaway fibres when working over a finished figure.

Waxed dental tape flat satin tape is good for jointing (see Little Dancer on page 82).

Bobble pins to position eyes and limbs.

Tape measure for measuring limbs and shapes.

Embroidery scissors curved for trimming and cutting fibres.

Straight scissors for shaping and trimming foam.

Bradawl to make holes for eyes and neck wires.

Knitting needles for knitting costumes and enlarging holes.

Tweezers to remove broken needles.

Barbeque sticks for rolling sausage shapes for limbs and for making accessories.

Modelling clay we like to model our sculptures before needle felting to work out the simple shapes that are needed (see Knitting Nigel clay model on page 25).

Polymer clay for making accessories.

Masking tape for securing armature wires.

Clear strong glue for securing wire and accessories, wrapping and details.

Glue gun and glue sticks for securing a finished project to a base.

Wire-backed dolls' eyes are available in different sizes from doll- and bear-making suppliers.

Cookie cutter, heart-shaped (see Queen of Hearts on page 66).

Chalk pastels for adding colour to features.

Craft knife for scraping pastel powder and for cutting foam shapes.

Small plastic containers for storing pastel powders.

Paintbrushes small and medium for applying pastels and for painting accessories and wooden bases.

Acid-free fixative for fixing pastel powder on a needle-felted surface.

Acrylic paints for painting accessories and wooden bases (see the Silver Surfer on page 126).

Thick black felt tipped pen for marking features.

Balsa wood for supporting the surfboard (see Silver Surfer on page 126).

Sandpaper for sanding accessories.

Embellishments buttons, beads, faceted gems, sequins, ribbon, lace, netting, scrim, miniature charms, paper and fabric flowers, ready-made felt.

Polystyrene ball many different shapes are available in craft stores, and you can needle felt straight on to the surface.

Wooden base for standing dolls, to complement finished projects.

Steam iron for ironing flat pieces.

Drill and drill bit 1.6mm ($\frac{1}{16}$in) for attaching a doll to a wooden base.

Small digital scales for weighing wool fibres.

Round-nosed pliers to bend the wire.

Wire cutters large and small for cutting different wire thicknesses.

Waxed floral tape for wrapping the wire glasses (see Weird and Wonderful on page 160).

Tools and materials for wet felting

An old towel to protect the work surface and roll the felt.

Bubble wrap to work on.

Netting to lay over the fibres.

Olive soap used when rubbing the fibres.

Laminate underlay used as a resist. You could also use thick acetate or thin plastic.

Cheese grater to grate the soap.

Bulb spray or a bottle with holes in the top to dribble water onto the fibres.

Rolling pin or a length of pipe insulation to roll the fibres.

Wet felting tool to help speed up the felting process.

Bowl to contain the soapy water.

Inspiration and design

You may want to design your own doll, but where and how would you start? Perhaps this idea is a little scary because you have never done it before, or you feel you are not at all creative. Don't worry, relax and approach things in easy stages. First get to know the needle felting method so that you understand what is possible. There is a helpful Getting started section on pages 28–31, then if you follow our Basic doll step-by-step instructions (see pages 32–47), you will learn how to create a male and a female figure. To encourage more play we have included ten projects (see pages 60–161) ranging from simple to more complex, showing how to develop a range of characters. Within these projects we have included variations, which illustrate how different colours and accessories can dramatically change the look of a doll.

As you progress through the book you will probably find that ideas will suddenly pop up while you are needling away. Make a note of them and gather together any thoughts you may have in a sketchbook or notepad. Even altering the size of ears or a nose can make a look your own. Changing hair colour can also have a dramatic effect, so let your imagination fly! We hope we give you the confidence to develop your own ideas by explaining what we do and how we do it in simple terms. Remember that there are no hard and fast rules, and if it works for you there is no right or wrong.

Sid the Silver Surfer, young at heart, dancing over the waves (see the project on page 118).

What inspires us

The wonderful thing about inspiration is that it can suddenly appear even when you are not actively thinking about it. We find that everyday things at home can spark off a thought, or ideas can happen when we are out driving or walking somewhere. It could be a dream or a favourite book that offers an exciting 'light bulb' moment. Occasionally we will think of a theme, as we did with our Silver Surfer. He was born because we wanted to include a project with an older character having a fun time. Ideas can also come from family and friends, or you might even want to do a 'selfie'. Capturing a realistic look is fun if you add accessories that tell the story of the person you are making.

Our longer car journeys have offered us great opportunities for inspired doodlings. We always return home with notebooks full of scribbles and sketches, some bordering on the ridiculous. We love to make people smile and humour is an important element in what we do. Knitting Nigel (opposite) sprang into life on one of these journeys. Names come easily once an idea is formed, and of course, being a knitaholic Nigel had to have a comfortable armchair too!

Capturing the look and personality of a friend or loved one is fun to do. Here we have made 'us' (see the project on page 128).

24

Developing the idea

Needle felting is all about the joining together of simple forms to create a character, so do study the shapes that make up a human body (see page 33). This will help you when you are developing an idea because it is all about simplifying the basics before adding character details.

So, how do we turn a doll doodle into reality? We find that it helps if we draw a further sketch to establish the size, colouring and character of the subject. This also helps us to identify the shapes that will make up the three-dimensional body. We will then sculpt what we have drawn using modelling clay, which allows us easily to change, take away, or add to a pose. As each doll transforms from its two-dimensional image to its three-dimensional form, the design will evolve until it feels just right. Even a slight upturn of the head or a tiny twist of a wrist can add instant appeal and charm. Proportions can be altered too, maybe elongating limbs or adding height. It is also fun to see how a personality can be enhanced with different accessories, or a change of clothes.

Here is Nigel's sister, Patchwork Pam. See how you can develop a different character by simply changing the colours you are using. In this way, and by mixing and matching the techniques, you can discover the magic of making your own original dolls.

Thinking about colours

Choosing colours is fun and we select them to complement and portray our dolls' 'stories'. On this page Mother Earth reflects nature in her soft greens, oranges and browns, while the Christmas Fairy (below) is seasonably white and crowned with a festive wreath of green and red. Kawaii Kate is cute in purple and Glorious Gloria is a vibrant delight. Each character is enhanced by the choices we make. It could be that further on, as you are needle felting, other colour ideas pop up. Great! It is all about following your intuition.

A doll is born

Now it is time to bring your doll to life. Despite having carefully planned things to this stage, the wool will be taking you on a delightful and surprising journey. As you needle felt the body, your character will probably start to take on its own personality. In workshops we have found that the students' personalities are reflected in the dolls they make. We have had blinged up beauties, leopard skin lovelies and golden oldies. We love this. If the same happens to you relax and just go with it. It is all part of the beauty and magic of the craft. Even if you are following our instructions very carefully your doll will become unique to you.

What we wear tells us so much about who we are, so choosing clothes is an important part of the design. We have received a lot of pleasure from needle felting and wet felting garments for our dolls. Go with the making flow and welcome all the surprises. Experiment with different colours, mix and match accessories, play with ideas and above all have fun!

Mother Earth's soft, natural colours are captured in her dress, shawl and headband (see the project on page 138).

Glorious Gloria, dynamic in all ways (see the project variation on page 127).

Kawaii Kate, cute in lilac and purple (see the project on page 106).

The Christmas Fairy, festive in seasonal colours (see the project on page 98).

Perfect poses

If you are designing your own dolls, poses and how they are achieved are important elements. We show three methods of making in the following pages: without an armature where the pose is static; with a partial armature where the doll's arms and legs can be moved into different poses; and with a full armature where the whole figure is more mobile. In each of the methods the pose decision has to be made early on. As you work through the projects you will understand the decision-making process more. It involves a whole series of questions that have to be answered, such as 'Do I want my doll to stand up without falling over?', 'Will the doll be active or passive?', or 'Do I want the arms to be moveable so it is able to hold something, or not?' Enjoy the learning process and you will soon be making these decisions as you become more familiar with the technique.

Storytelling

Storytelling is a big part of what we do and adding accessories can immediately relay the personality of a doll. If you are designing your own dolls, think about the stories you want to tell as the characters develop, then jot down some ideas about the extras you might add to portray their passions and interests.

If you choose to follow our instructions through the book and learn all the different techniques, you may want to pop into another project, pick an appropriate accessory and add it to the story you are telling. Our woolly witch carries a book that is featured in a later project (see page 160). By simply changing the colour it has been transformed into an ancient book of spells. Her companion crow is a black version of Mother Earth's white doves (see opposite), and the instructions for her cauldron are similar to those given for planet Earth. Mixing and matching in this way will create different characters and it is a fun part of the design process.

Our Woolly Witch loves making magic, rarely leaving her forest home without her precious spell book. Her crow is a constant companion, helping to brew potent potions in a cauldron fired by dragon's breath.

Getting started

We use two techniques in our book: needle felting and wet felting. Needle felting, also known as dry felting, is the method used to create the dolls. We use wet felting to create the beautiful delicate fabrics for their clothes. We love being able to combine the two techniques, especially in our doll making where clothes and accessories play such an important part in the portrayal of each character.

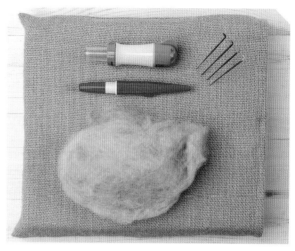

The basic needle felting materials needed to start one of our projects.

Are you sitting comfortably?

Where and how you work is important. It is all about feeling relaxed and enjoying what you are doing. The working areas needed for the two felting techniques are very different. Needle felting takes up very little space as you only work with one pad, some wool and needles. Wet felting involves laying out fibres and energetic rubbing and rolling, so more space is needed.

Needle felting

When needle felting you will be stabbing wool with a needle to felt the fibres so there will be long sitting periods. From experience we know this can lead to aches and pains, so do make your workspace comfortable. A cushioned chair is a good idea! We have hydraulic chairs so that we can alter the height and this helps prevent backache. You will also need a sturdy work table, a foam pad, felting needles and your wool. The repetitive stabbing can become addictive, so take frequent tea and biscuit breaks and quick wanders around to loosen up. Working in good daylight is ideal, but if your natural light is restricted, or you are needling away in the evening, you can buy daylight bulbs that really help. While working you should always focus on what you are doing to avoid stabbing yourself. Watching television when concentrating on a project can be a recipe for disaster. We love listening to the radio instead.

Wet felting

Quite a bit of water is used in wet felting so you need to give yourself enough room to work comfortably. Prepare a large work table before you start. Lay down an old towel with a piece of bubble wrap, bubbles facing up. Have ready a piece of netting, a bowl of warm water, olive soap, a water sprinkler, a grater, a felting tool, a length of pipe insulation and your wool.

The wet felting materials we use to make some of our dolls' clothes.

How it works

Needle felting looks very easy. 'All you do is stab', we hear students say. Yes, there is a lot of stabbing involved, but there is much more to it than that. Attacking the wool as though the needle is a pneumatic drill will not produce the best results. Frenzied poking will only lead to broken needles and probably pricked fingers. It is far better to take it easy and remember, needle felting is not a quick craft. Our students are often surprised how long a project can take. For us, however, this slow repetitive technique is wonderfully therapeutic. In a frantic world, working with wool in this way can have a really calming effect, so slow down and enjoy the process.

Holding the felting needle

Get comfortable, relax and grip the needle firmly but not so tight that it could cause you to seize up! Place your thumb at the front of the needle with two fingers behind it to support it as you work. Stabbing should be rhythmical with a relaxed arm. It is more of a wrist movement when you are working, rather than a whole arm movement, so start off resting your hand in a comfortable position on the edge of the pad.

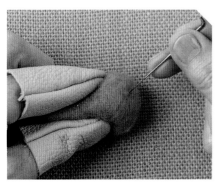
Using a single needle.

Using a three-needle tool.

> ## Woolly warnings
>
> Take care when using felting needles. They are extremely sharp so keep some plasters handy!
>
> We advise that children under ten should be supervised by an adult when needle felting.
>
> Some pets, especially dogs, love wool and anything needle felted, so keep everything in a safe place.

Away we go

Everything we create is made up of simple shapes and each one will require the same considered approach. Here we show you how the subtleties are important, what to do when and how to do it. This will apply to everything you make. Needle felting goes through different stages as you work. If you can recognize them it will help you understand what is going on. Do not worry, as you become more experienced it will all become instinctive. Once we have covered the essentials, we can us have some fun.

Templates

Actual-sized templates for all the dolls are at the back of the back of the book (see pages 162–175). The outlines show the size and shape of the different felted parts that are needed to create the dolls and their accessories. Most of the shapes are three-dimensional. Where they are flat this is indicated within the template outlines.

You can measure the amount of wool needed for each body part using these templates. Wool shrinks by approximately a third as you felt it. If it is rolled a third larger than the template outline it will needle felt down to the correct size (see below).

However, throughout the book we have given you wool weights for all the body parts and accessories, so rather than measuring the wool you may prefer to purchase some small digital scales like those pictured above.

The templates show the size and shape that make up the dolls and their accessories. The fringed lines on the outlines indicate where loose fibres should be left so that one shape can be attached to another.

Using the templates

Here we show how to use the template and how to attach one shape to another.

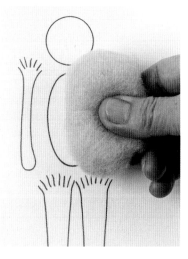

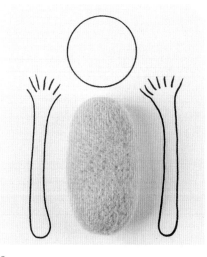

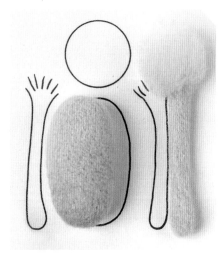

1 Take some wool and roll it tightly until it is one third larger than the torso shape on the template.

2 Once needle felted the wool will shrink down to the size of the template.

3 Needle felt an arm, leaving loose fibres at the top for attaching.

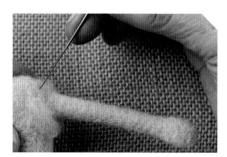

4 Splay out the fibres, press the arm on the body and needle to secure.

Stages of working

Opposite we needle felt a 4cm (1½in) diameter ball to explain how needle felting works when working on a larger shape, and how long each stage will take. For smaller and more intricate shapes like feet and hands we use a single needle and this technique can be seen in the basic doll instructions (see pages 32–39).

It is much easier to needle felt soft, fluffy fibres, so if your wool is lumpy or matted you may want to card it first (see page 13).

If you are new to needle felting do spend a little time here, then you can progress on to making the basic doll.

Tip

Beware the air when you are rolling the wool to start off a shape. Expel as much air as possible and roll the fibres tightly. This is important because it will speed up the felting process – you do not want to be needling thin air.

Order of working for larger shapes

Generally, for larger body parts we work as below. Single needles are used when we create smaller more intricate shapes and these are explained individually.

1. Three-needle tool to start the process.

2. 40 triangle needle to refine the shape.

3. Five-needle tool to speed up the process.

4. 40 triangle needle to tidy up the shape.

5. 40 twisted needle to smooth the surface.

Roll the shape between your hands frequently throughout.

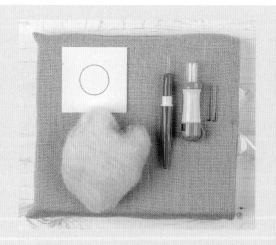

1 Roll the wool into a tight ball to expel the air.

2 Plunge the three-needle tool deeply and evenly into and around the ball until it retains its shape without the fibres springing out (5 minutes).

What you need

- Foam pad
- Coarse wool: 5g (⅙oz)
- Three-needle tool
- Felting needles: 40 triangle, 40 twisted
- Five-needle tool

3 Continue with the 40 triangle needle until the ball shrinks down and the surface starts to dimple. We call this the 'cellulite' stage and it is a good sign that the inside of the ball is needle felted (5 minutes).

4 Roll the ball between the palms of your hands. This will smooth the surface and speed up the felting process. When felting, wool loves a little friction! (1 minute).

Tips

If you do not have the multi-needle tools, you can use the 40 triangle needle instead. It will just take more time.

You will only achieve a smooth surface if the felting beneath is completely firm. Once needled smooth you can work over the shapes with a fuzz removing tool or trim flyaway fibres with curved embroidery scissors.

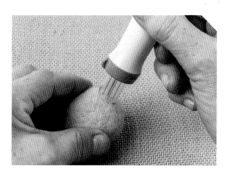

5 Now work over the ball with the five-needle tool. This will shrink the ball further and smooth the surface a little more (3 minutes).

6 For more control use a 40 triangle needle and make shallow, even stabs all over to smooth the surface, until it matches the template size (5 minutes).

7 Use the twisted needle and pin prick the whole surface with your needle at an angle to tuck away any flyaway fibres (5 minutes).

Total time: 24 minutes

Basic doll

simple shapes ✳ no armature

Whether large or small, simple or complex, the method behind needle felting is the same. It is all about making and joining shapes whether you are creating a doll, a book or a sheep. These shapes are the building blocks for your characters and once you have learnt how to control and sculpt the wool your imagination can take flight. This is why we love the craft so.

   The following step-by-step instructions (see pages 34–39) will ease you into the doll-making process. We simplify shapes by thinking of a head as a ball, a body as an oval and a leg or arm as a sausage, and this makes the anatomy far less scary. So, once you have completed this section you can add to your knowledge by working through the projects. Alternatively, if you feel more confident, you can open a page, jump in and have fun. But for now, let's start with the basics.

Basic body shapes

Here we teach you how to make simple doll shapes (see below) and build them up in easy stages. It is an exciting journey and one that we look forward to sharing with you.

Accessories and clothes

We love accessorizing our dolls because this helps to tell their stories. As with the dolls, these accessories are all based on simple shapes and we show how to needle felt hats and a bag on the following pages. Creating a woolly wardrobe for each character is an exciting moment and the wet felting technique offers great opportunities for developing garment ideas. So we also show how to wet felt a simple skirt and a more complex shirt using the resist method.

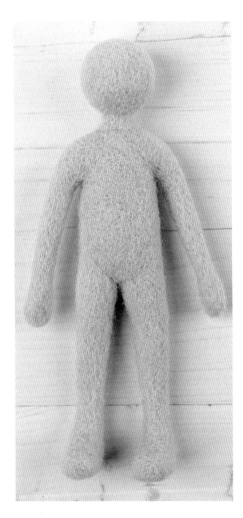

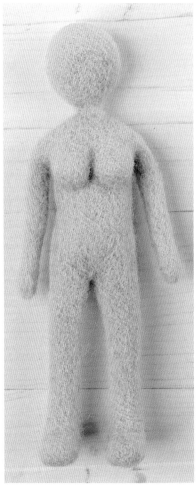

Template
Actual size

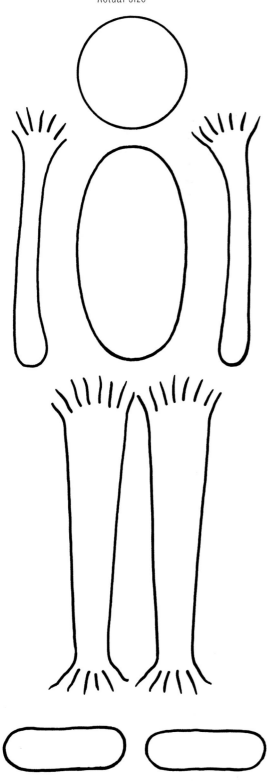

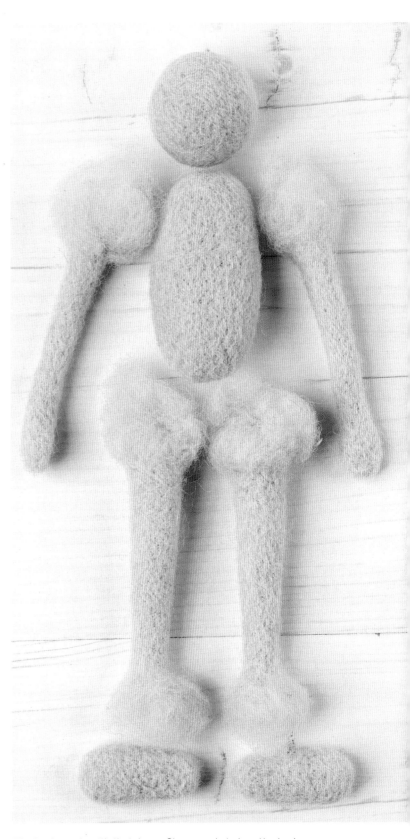

The body parts with their loose fibres ready to be attached.

Needle felting the figures

First set up your workspace, get comfortable and relax (see page 28). The male doll is made using simple three-dimensional shapes. The female doll is made the same but with woolly breasts. The dolls are 16cm (6¼in) tall.

Important needle notes to remember

• To prevent stabbing yourself, always work on your pad, never in mid-air!

• Beware the air. Always roll your wool tightly otherwise you will be needling thin air.

• Do not bend the needle. It should go straight into the fibres and straight out with no wriggling about inside the shape, otherwise your needle will break! Always keep the same angle.

• Remember to relax and do not use the needle like a pneumatic drill.

• Work all over the shape evenly and methodically.

Our needle code

We have colour-coded our needles so that you can easily identify them in the step-by-step photographs.

● 40 triangle – red
● 38 triangle – blue
● 36 triangle – yellow
● 40 twisted – green

···· **What you need** ····

• Templates on page 33 for size and shape
• Carded coarse wool: 15g (½oz) flesh coloured
• Foam pad
• Three-needle tool
• Felting needles: 40 triangle, 40 twisted
• Five-needle tool
• Barbeque stick
• Bradawl
• Thick wire: 6cm (2½in) length of 1.6mm (16 gauge)
• Wire cutters
• Strong clear glue
• Curved embroidery scissors

Ball head

You will need a small amount of coarse wool, the three-needle tool, a 40 triangle needle and a 40 twisted needle.

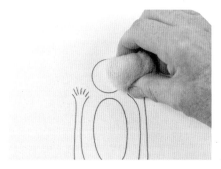

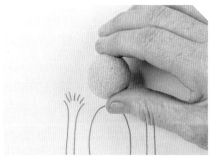

1 Roll 2.5g (1/12oz) of wool into a tight ball. It will be one third larger than the template.

2 Needle felt the ball working through the different stages (see page 31) until it shrinks down to match the template.

3 To finish, smooth the surface using the twisted needle.

Oval body

You will need 4.5g (⅙oz) of coarse wool, a five-needle tool, a 40 triangle needle and a 40 twisted needle.

1 Lay 4.5g (⅙oz) of wool on the pad, then fold the sides in.

2 Roll the fibres into a tight sausage.

3 Needle one end round and firm using a 40 triangle needle.

4 Turn the oval round and needle the other end in the same way. At this point the oval will be larger than the template.

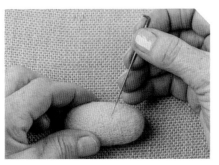

5 Now needle felt to the cellulite stage, then follow steps 4–7 on page 31 to shrink the oval and smooth the surface.

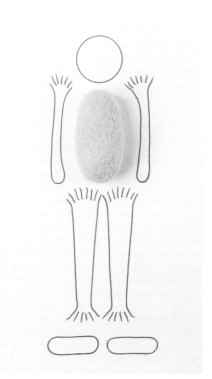

Tips

Always needle felt the shapes firmly so that when they are attached together they do not loosen over time. This is particularly important if you want your dolls to stand up.

If you are needle felting smaller shapes, like feet and hands, use a single needle, as the shapes are too small to be worked on with the multi-needle tools.

Sausage arms

You will need a barbecue stick, a small amount of coarse wool, a 40 triangle needle and a 40 twisted needle.

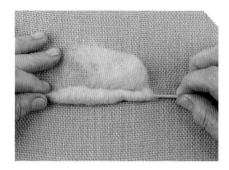

1 Roll a small amount of wool tightly around a barbecue stick.

2 Remove the stick gently and using the 40 triangle needle stab one end round to create the hand.

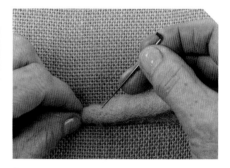

3 Turn the arm and use the needle to 'pack' the wool into the hand.

4 Roll the wool between your hands to continue the felting.

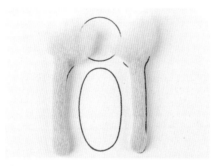

5 Continue needling the remaining wool sausage until it matches the template, leaving loose ends for attaching. Use the twisted needle to smooth and finish (see page 31). Repeat.

Tip

When 'packing' the wool, angle the needle towards where you want the fibres to be and gently poke them into position.

Graduated sausage legs

You will need a barbecue stick, 2g ($\frac{1}{16}$oz) of coarse wool, a 40 triangle needle and a 40 twisted needle.

1 Roll 2g ($\frac{1}{16}$oz) of wool tightly around a barbeque stick then remove the stick. Using the 40 triangle needle, start needling the ankle leaving loose ends for attaching the foot.

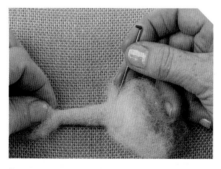

2 Turn the leg round. As you needle, 'pack' the lower leg with the wool fibres to firm it up and pack more wool to widen it as you work up towards the thigh.

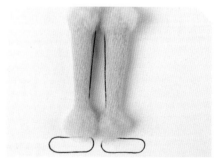

3 When it matches the template size, leave loose fibres at the top for attaching to the body. Use the twisted needle to smooth and finish (see page 31). Repeat.

Small flattened sausage feet

You will need a barbecue stick, a small amount of coarse wool, a 40 triangle needle and a 40 twisted needle.

1 Roll a small amount of wool tightly around the stick, then remove the stick.

2 Needle felt the wool using the 40 triangle needle, rounding the ends until the sausage matches the template.

3 Needle into one side to flatten slightly.

4 When it matches the template use the twisted needle to smooth and finish. Repeat.

Joining the shapes together

You will need a 40 triangle needle, a bradawl, 6cm (2½in) of thick wire, wire cutters, glue, a 38 triangle needle and a 40 twisted needle.

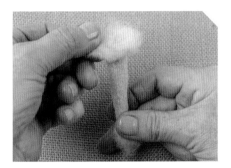  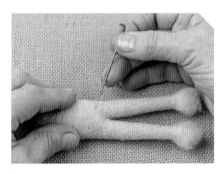

1 Carefully splay out the fibres at the top of one leg.

2 Press it firmly onto the body and needle felt the loose fibres using the 40 triangle needle.

3 Attach the other leg, then needle the body to a smooth finish with the twisted needle.

 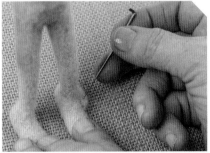 

4 Repeat this process to attach the two arms.

5 Splay out the fibres on the legs and press the feet in place. Needle felt the loose fibres of the leg into the foot using the 40 triangle needle. Smooth and finish with the twisted needle.

6 Use a bradawl to make a hole in the head and one in the body.

7 Glue and insert the wire into the body. Glue the other wire end and push the head into place, leaving 1cm (½in) of wire visible for the neck.

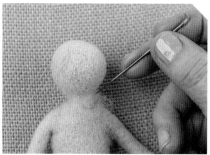

8 Wrap the wire loosely with a little more wool and use a 38 triangle needle to felt the fibres into the body and the head.

Tip

The 38 triangle needle is thicker than the 40 gauge needles and therefore stronger. You should always use stronger needles when working near wire. We use the 38 triangle needle when working with partial armatures like this, and the 36 triangle when working with a full armature.

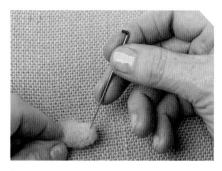

9 Female doll For a girl doll you can add breasts. Needle felt a small ball of wool leaving loose fibres on one side.

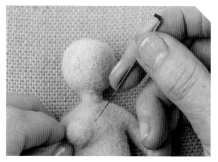

10 Splay out the loose fibres and press one ball onto the body. Needle felt to secure.

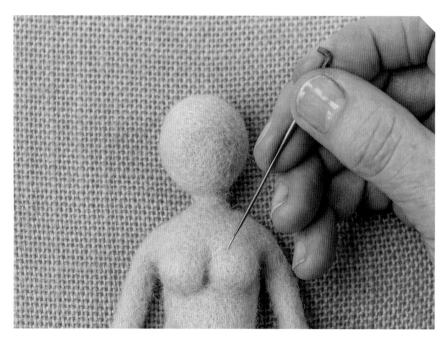

11 Sculpt a smooth slope above and a rounded shape below, using the 40 twisted needle. Repeat.

Tip

Remember that gravity means the breasts will sag with age and sit lower on the chest.

Shaping up

At this stage you may want to build up areas of the body, such as the tummy, buttocks, shoulders or breasts. You will need a 40 triangle needle, a 40 twisted needle and embroidery scissors.

1 To add buttocks to the doll lay some fibres on the pad. Needle them softly in the centre leaving loose fibres all around.

2 Lay the semi-felted shape over the lower back of the doll and needle the loose fibres in to secure, then smooth the surface with the twisted needle (see page 31).

3 Still using the twisted needle, work over the doll to smooth and finish.

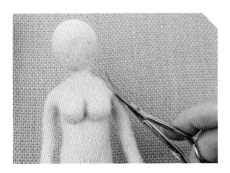

4 Trim any flyaway fibres with embroidery scissors.

The finished basic figures

The shapes and joining method shown on these pages form the basis for all the dolls that we make. With extra 'padding' these shapes can be accentuated and built on. Now we move on to more shape making as we show you how to add clothes and accessories.

Other useful shapes

On these pages you will need small amounts of coarse wool, a 40 triangle needle and a 40 twisted needle.

Box

A square with a needle-felted strap makes a handy shoulder bag.

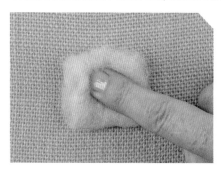

1 Lay a small amount of wool on the pad and fold the edges in to create a small square.

2 Needle the square, using a 40 triangle needle, until the wool binds together. Flip and repeat this a few times.

3 Needle each flat edge, one at a time, to neaten.

4 Keep working in this way until the square is really firm and the edges are sharp. Neaten with a 40 twisted needle.

Template

Actual size

Strap

You do not need many fibres to make a strap. A towel will help to speed up the felting.

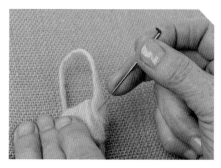

1 Lay a thin 10cm (4in) length of wool on the pad. Needle felt the length using the 40 triangle needle. Flip and repeat this a few times.

2 Roll firmly between wet hands and on a towel until it is felted.

3 Attach the strap to the bag by needling the ends into the square.

Cone

A simple cone makes a great hat for Father Christmas (see page 67).

1 Lay a small amount of wool on the pad. Fold in one side to make it thicker.

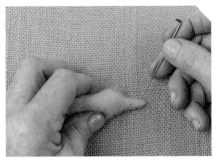

2 Roll the fibres up tightly and needle felt the thinner end using a 40 triangle needle.

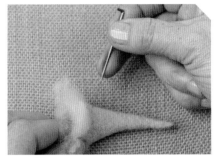

3 Needle felt the rest of the shape to create the cone. Work down the shape so that it thickens, leaving loose fibres on the end.

Cylinder

An ideal shape for a top hat (see page 159).

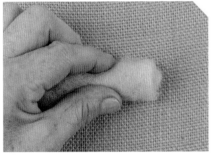

1 Roll 2g (¹⁄₁₆oz) of wool into a thick, tight sausage and needle it lightly to secure.

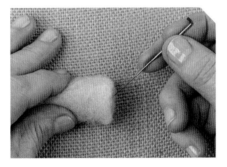

2 Needle felt one end flat using the 40 triangle needle.

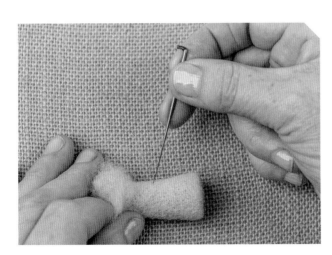

3 Work down the shape so that it matches the template (see right), leaving loose fibres as shown.

Templates

Actual size

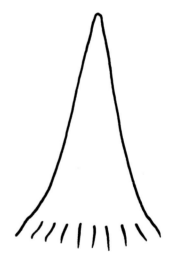

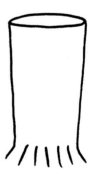

Flat circle

Flat shapes can be needle felted or wet felted. A circle makes an excellent hat brim and this needs to be fairly firm, so we have chosen to needle felt the shape. Wet-felted pieces are more delicate and are better used as part of an outfit. A smoother finish can be achieved if you steam iron a needle-felted flat shape: use a wool setting leaving loose fibres free. Trim any felted edges with embroidery scissors.

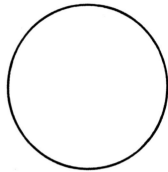

1 Arrange a small amount of fibres in a circle on the pad with the tip of a 40 triangle needle. Needle shallowly to firm up.

2 Flip and repeat this a few times and then use the five-needle tool to continue the felting process.

3 Rub the felt circle between your hands, then work around the edge of the circle tucking in the loose fibres to neaten. Trim away any leftover loose fibres with embroidery scissors and steam iron.

Making a hat with the flat circle and cylinder

Place the cylinder (see previous page) on top of the circle and needle the loose fibres into the brim until secure and smooth.

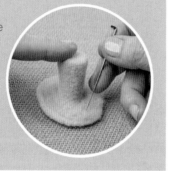

Tip

When neatening edges you can protect your fingers by using a piece of folded card if preferred (see step 2 below).

Flat strip

We use this versatile strip for boot collars, sleeves and shorts. Here we are making a boot collar. Flip the strip a few times as you work, to ensure even felting.

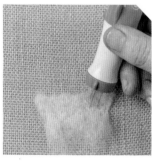

1 Lay a small amount of wool on the pad. Use the tip of the 40 triangle needle to straighten the top and sides. Needle the strip leaving the loose fibres free, then use the five-needle tool.

2 Hold the strip loosely between your fingers and needle along the three felted edges to neaten.

3 Wrap it around the ankle and needle the loose fibres into the foot.

Wet felting the skirt and shirt

The needle felting technique is fine for clothes that are close fitting and permanent, but if you want to create free flowing or removeable garments the wet felting technique is better. Water, friction and heat are the key ingredients needed to create impressive clothes and the method is great fun.

When making flat pieces for dresses, if you combine wool with silks wonderfully organic results can be achieved (see page 147). More complex clothes can be created as well. The skirt (below) and the shirt (see pages 45–47) are made using two techniques. The skirt is a flat circle with a hole in the middle for the doll to slip into. The shirt is removeable and is made using the resist method. We find that foam underlay for laminate flooring is ideal as a resist, but flexible thick acetate or thin plastic is just as good.

As you work the wool will shrink and become firmer, so when planning a piece this has to be taken into consideration.

What you need

- Old towel
- Bubble wrap
- Small amount of Merino wool
- Netting
- Grater
- Olive soap
- Bulb spray (or an old plastic bottle with holes in the top)
- Wet felting tool
- Dressmaking scissors
- Rolling pin or a length of pipe insulation
- Bowl
- 40 twisted needle

Tip

When using Merino wool for wet felting, pull the fibres gently, with an even tension. Grasp the ends of the fibres with a closed fist to give you a fine layer.

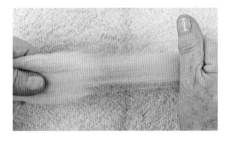

Skirt

First, set up your wet felting workspace (see page 28).

1 On top of the bubble wrap (bubbles up) lay radiating wisps of Merino wool in a 10cm (4in) circle, overlapping them for a good coverage.

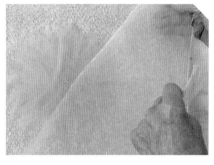

2 Gently cover the wool with a piece of netting. This will keep the fibres in place while felting.

3 Grate some olive soap into a bowl of hot water and use the bulb spray or bottle to dribble this over the netting. Make sure the fibres are wetted thoroughly.

4 Rub the surface with the soap bar, then rub it gently with the palms of your hands. Keep rubbing in different directions, gradually pressing harder until the fibres felt together and become stable. Now gently use your wet felting tool.

5 Gently peel off the netting. Flip the felt over and continue rubbing with your hands. Once the fibres are felted they will be firmly knitted together. If there are any loose fibres you will need to rub a little longer to ensure that the wool is fully felted.

6 Trim the circle with scissors to neaten, then rub the soapy felt circle between your hands for a few minutes.

7 Place the felt on the bubble wrap with the roller on top. Roll up the bubble wrap with the felt enclosed.

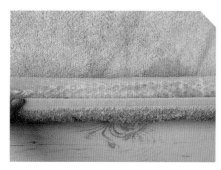

8 Roll the towel around the bubble wrap. Roll 50 times, unroll, move the skirt around 45 degrees. Roll in the bubble wrap and towel again, and roll another 50 times.

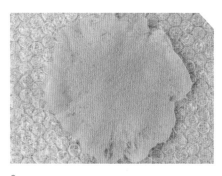

9 Repeat the previous step twice more, then flip the skirt and repeat. This will cause it to shrink and firm up. Unroll and remove the felted circle.

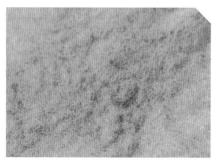

10 Wash the felt in hot water to remove the soap, then rinse in cold water and throw it repeatedly onto a hard surface to 'shock' the fibres. This gives a wonderful organic textured feel to the felt.

11 Fold the circle into four. Cut across the folded top point approximately 1cm (½in) down.

13 When dry, needle around the top of the skirt with the twisted needle to shrink the waistband so it fits the waist. Smooth the waist area to finish.

12 Slide it over the doll's legs up to her waist and arrange the skirt folds. Leave to dry.

Shirt

First, set up your wet felting workspace (see page 28).

Template

Actual size

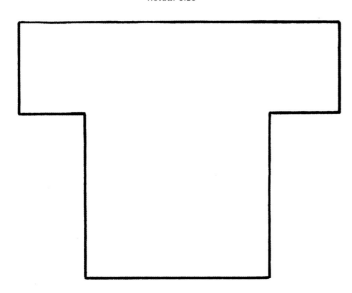

What you need

- For the resist, a piece of foam underlay, thick acetate or thin plastic
- Ballpoint pen
- Old towel
- Bubble wrap
- Merino wool: 5g (⅙oz)
- Netting
- Grater
- Olive soap
- Bulb spray (or an old plastic bottle with holes in the top)
- Dressmaking scissors
- Wet felting tool
- Rolling pin or a length of pipe insulation
- Bowl

1 Lay the resist over the template and trace over the outline. Cut out the shape.

2 Place the resist towards one side of your bubble wrap and cover it with thin overlapping wisps of Merino wool. Let the fibres trail over the outer edges. Lay another thin layer at right angles to the first and a third layer at right angles to the second.

3 Gently cover the wool with the netting to hold the fibres in place. Wet the wool with warm soapy water (see step 3 on page 43).

4 Fold the bubble wrap over to cover all the wool on the working area.

5 Flip the folded bubble wrap over and open it up.

6 Cut into the corners so that the underarm fibres can lie flat before folding the fibres onto the resist.

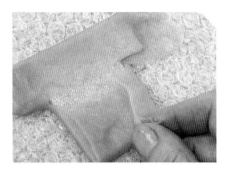

7 Carefully fold the rest of the outer wet fibres onto the resist.

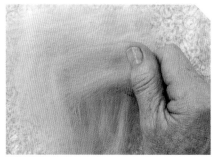

8 Cover this side of the resist with three layers of wool as before.

9 Fold and flip the bubble wrap then fold the overhanging fibres on to the resist, cutting into the arms as before (see step 6).

10 Lay the netting over the resist and rub with your hands, gently at first then more firmly as the fibres bind together. Rub for five minutes on this side. Repeat on the other side then use the wet felting tool to speed up the process.

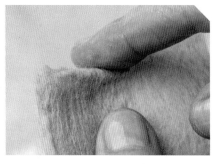

11 Rub between your hands, especially up and down the edges of the resist to make sure they have felted.

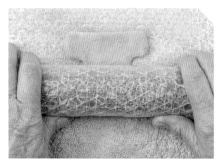

12 Repeat the rolling technique in steps 7–9 on page 44.

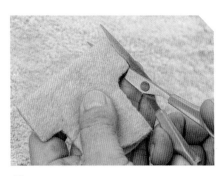

13 Cut along the bottom of the shirt and across the ends of the sleeves.

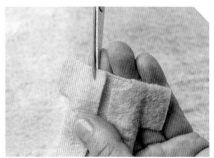

14 Cut up the centre and then cut a 2cm (¾in) semi-circle across the front neck edge.

15 Carefully remove the resist.

16 Rub along the shoulders, under the arms and down the sides of the shirt to smooth.

17 Wash the shirt in hot water, squeeze to remove excess water then check the shape. Trim any untidy edges.

18 Finally, wash in cold water, wring out. While still wet, fit the shirt to your figure, arrange it and leave to dry.

The basic doll instructions can be used as a springboard for your own characters using different ideas shown in the projects (see pages 62–161). Here you can see the basic doll with her wet-felted skirt. The teeny doll she is holding is made by reducing the basic doll template by two thirds.

Top 'help me' tips

After many years of teaching we have seen some marvellous mistakes! Needle felting has its moments when things do not quite go as planned, but do not worry as most errors can be corrected. These tips will help you out of a woolly hole.

Crinkly crevices

Oh no, a bumpy, crevice-like fold! Do not worry. Sometimes when you are rolling the wool tightly this happens as the fibres start binding together. It is easier to put things right sooner rather than later. If the fold is shallow, see below. If it is deep, just cover the area with extra fibres and gently needle until smooth.

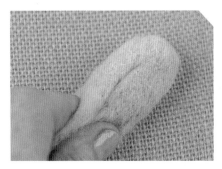

1 A crevice appears.

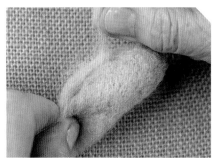

2 Pull out the fibres to loosen them.

3 With the needle at an angle, gently needle the fibres back into the surface.

Pancake limbs

You may have heard the expression 'flat as a pancake'. This happens when sausage limbs are not needled evenly all the way round as you work up and down the shape. Only working on one side of the shape will flatten the fibres. Roll the sausage as you needle to achieve an even, rounded finish.

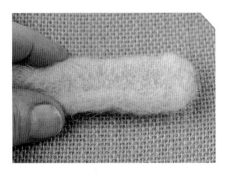

1 Feeling flat?

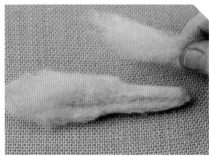

2 Roll the shape in your hands and add fibres to any crevices.

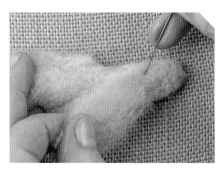

3 Gently needle the fibres back into the surface until smooth.

Horrible holes

If you needle an area over and over in the same place, the wool will shrink and a hole will appear. You may want this to happen if you are creating eye sockets or dimples, but if you want a smooth surface what do you do?

1 Oh no, a hole!

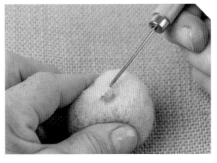

2 Use a bradawl to pull out some fibres. Add fibres if the hole is deep.

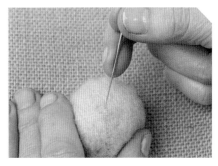

3 Gently needle the fibres back into the surface until smooth.

Puffy peaks

Puffy peaks happen when you work unevenly and needle felt some areas more than others. There will be hard and soft areas resulting in a lumpy bumpy surface.

1 No doll wants puffy peaks!

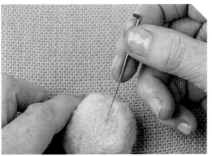

2 Needle into softer peaks to remove the air and flatten the fibres.

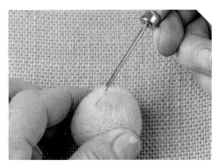

3 Fibres in harder areas can be loosened with a bradawl and gently reworked as for horrible holes, above.

Size matters

If a shape is too small, add a layer of wool and carry on needle felting. A more drastic remedy is needed if a shape is too big. Normally we would not be telling you to cut fibres because the results can be blunt and unattractive. However, occasionally you may have to do this. We have carried out a few major operations on our woolly families over the years, even amputations and decapitations!

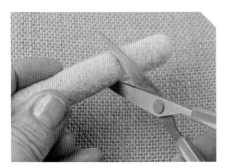

1 Too big? Time to amputate!

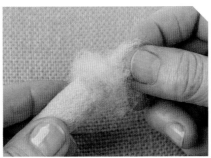

2 Layer fibres over the cut wound.

3 Needle them in and around the area to create a smooth surface.

Creating an inner core

Needle felting a large shape in coarse wool can take a long time. If you make a central core using inexpensive core wool it will save time and therefore speed up the shape-making process. The more costly wools can then be worked on top. We normally make a core when a shape is bigger than a hen's egg. When it is smaller, it is easier to use just coarse wool.

Core wool is available from most needle felting suppliers and some specialist craft stores. You can purchase it in different forms but we prefer to use rovings (long lengths) as they are perfect for wrapping and knotting an inner core.

What you need

- Core wool: round core 40g (1½oz), long core 20g (¾oz)
- Yarn
- Three-needle tool
- Five-needle tool
- 40 triangle needle
- 40 twisted needle

Making and covering a core

Cores should be slightly smaller than the template outline of the shape you are making. We have used two core methods in the projects, as shown here. One is for more rounded shapes, and the other is for longer, thinner shapes.

Round core

The same method applies to an oval shape.

1 Roll the core wool into a tight ball to remove all the air.

2 Wrap tightly with yarn to secure the shape and then needle any irregular bumps flat with the three-needle tool.

3 Lay the covering fibres loosely over the surface and stab them deeply and evenly into the core. Keep adding wool until the whole ball is covered.

4 Use the five-needle tool and work over the shape a few times until the surface is even.

5 Work over the surface with the 40 triangle needle several times, then pin prick the surface at an angle with the 40 twisted needle for a smooth finish.

Long core

A longer shape is more difficult to roll and wrap with yarn, so we prefer to use this method to create a firm inner core.

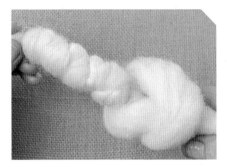

1 Tie knots closely together to form a long length.

2 Wrap more core wool tightly around the knotted length, to build up and strengthen the shape. Then wrap with yarn.

3 Work over the shape to even it up with the three-needle tool, then follow steps 3 and 4 opposite.

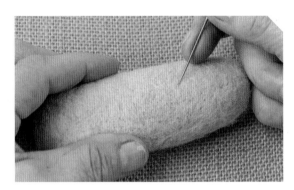

4 Finish by working over the surface with the 40 triangular needle several times, then pin prick the surface at an angle with the 40 twisted needle for a smooth finish.

Two inner cores are used for Kawaii Kate (see the project on pages 106–117). A round core is used for her head. For her body, the lower half of a long core is wrapped with extra core wool to create the pear shape before it is wrapped with yarn to secure.

Armatures

An armature is a frame that supports the figure. We use wire to create the basic structure and wool is wrapped around it to create the body shape. We have often been asked why an armature is necessary and when it should be used. The answer is not straightforward. Some of our characters are worked without any wire, some have partial frames and others have top to toe armatures. So, let us consider why we made these choices.

No armature

It is far easier to make a doll without an armature because you do not have to worry about hitting the wire and breaking your needle. However, occasionally we will insert a short wire into a neck if we want extra support and more flexibility for the head, as we have chosen to do with Patchwork Pam. If a doll is mainly unwired, its pose will be fixed and the body parts have to be needle felted very firmly so that the figure is strong enough to hold that position. With a standing doll without an armature, like Daisy, the legs have to be really firm and thick enough to support the upper body. A thinner doll, like Patchwork Pam, would have to be seated, or posed in a way that provides a stable base.

Patchwork Pam and Daisy.

Partial armature

With a partial armature we needle felt the head and body first without the worry of hitting any wire with the needle. If we start this way we can use an inner core to speed up the process. The head is then attached to the body with a short wire so that it can be posed at different angles. We also thread wires through the body to create the arms and legs – as on the Christmas Fairy – and these are then wrapped with wool. Dolls made this way can have thin arms and legs and the figures can be posed easily. Occasionally we will only wire the head, or the head and arms. Cute Caroline has her neck and arms wired, while her unwired legs are sturdy enough for her to stand on her own two feet.

The Christmas Fairy and Cute Caroline.

Top to toe armature

We do not often make a doll with a full armature because of the difficulties of needle felting around wire. However, occasionally we will decide to create one, when making a taller character like Mother Earth, because the doll will be stronger, it will stand unsupported and it can be re-posed easily. There are fewer templates if you choose this method because the felting process is much more organic. Wool is wound around the wire frame to create the figure's centre, then the body is gradually built up on top.

   If the doll is free-standing the feet must be big enough and sturdy enough to carry the body weight. Alternatively, the doll can be attached to a base for stability. The doll can still be posed and you do not have to think about balancing the figure.

When you are thinking about poses, you can sketch different positions first. Once the armature has been made you can experiment to see which pose works best.

Creating character and expression

Let's face it

The needle felting technique is great for capturing personality, mood and age. Even the simplest of features can add a touch of humour, or capture a certain look.

How do you create character and expression? It is easy enough to make a basic doll, but how do you turn it into a character with its own personality? The answer is in the face and body shape, the features, a pose, the clothes, the story that is being told, or a combination of all these elements. Our projects have been specially designed to take you from simple beginnings right through to sculpting realistic faces and features. They include a mix of styles with different body shapes and skin tones, so you can progress through the book to build up your skills, dip in and get going, or select and match favourite elements to create your own dolls.

Just two small beads for eyes, a cone nose and a sweet smile. A simple royal for our first project (see page 63).

Realistic eyes are made bigger here. With a button nose and cupid lips Caroline's cute look is complete (see page 117).

Add eyebrows, glasses and a big smile. Sally Strangelove is looking good (see page 161).

Capturing age

We show how to needle felt younger and older characters.

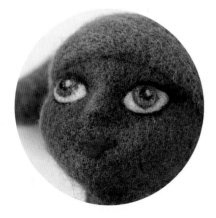

Kawaii Kate's baby face and youthful skin have been 'smoothed' to a fine finish (see page 107).

More realistic face sculpting for young at heart Roz (see page 137).

Older Silver Surfer Sid, with his needled laughter lines, loves having fun (see page 119).

Adding colour

We use pastel powder to 'blush' and colour skin because it gives a gentle, natural look. Alternatively you could use a felt tip pen, or gently needle in a few fibres of coarse wool to cover the area. For cheeks, use a blended mix of flesh-coloured and pale pink wool, then gently needle the fibres into the face.

Pretty in pastels

Pastel chalks can be purchased individually or in sets from art and craft stores. A fine powder is created if you gently scrape the surface of the pastel with a craft knife, and this can be applied to the needle-felted surface using a small paintbrush. Go gently if you want a delicate blush or apply more powder to achieve a deeper colour. When you are happy with the result, lightly spray painted areas with acid-free fixative. This seals the powder and stops it fading with handling.

Small sealed containers are ideal for storage if you want to use the powder colours again.

This little dancer has a natural blush of pastel colour on her cheeks (see page 83).

Well done Gloria! You have managed to put your eyeshadow on without smudging it (see page 127).

Mother Earth loves nature and natural colours, and her green fingers help the flowers, plants and trees to grow and flourish (see page 139).

Features

Getting the features right is one of the most important elements in doll making. The size and shape of eyes, noses, ears and mouths give very different looks and can really enhance or alter a doll's character.

Eyes

Glass and plastic eyes are available in many colours, shapes and sizes. We use wire-backed glass eyes and they can be purchased online, or you can buy them from doll and teddy bear suppliers. You can also needle felt eyes directly on to a doll's face with amazingly realistic results.

Adding colour

For our simpler dolls we use black wire-backed eyes. For more realistic dolls we buy clear wire-backed glass eyes then paint them. Acrylic paints can be brushed onto the back of the eyes, allowing more colour choices. If you want to paint and store your eyes for future use we advise that you allow the paint to dry, then add a protective coat of varnish. Otherwise, secure the eyes in the doll's head once the paint has dried.

Danny Doodoll's glass eyes are a simple choice, selected because they enhance his simple cartoon-like look (see page 69).

We have used clear glass eyes and painted them blue (see above right) to reflect Judy's eye colour.

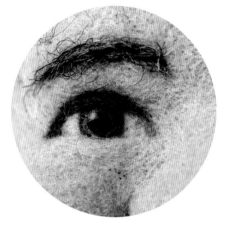

Creating a needle-felted eye is both challenging and fun. Eyebrows, eyelids, and the dot of light in the eye add to the realism and bring the eye to life (see page 155).

Tip

Have fun with bobble pins by trying out a variety of eye positions. Where they are placed can give very different looks.

Noses

The shape and size of this feature can make a huge difference to the look of a character. Learn how to create different noses starting with a simple cone shape and progressing on to a realistic sculpted nose with nostrils.

Mouths

As with noses, a mouth can enhance or change a look. We have included different shapes in the projects, starting with a simple single smile line and progressing on to more realistic full lips and teeth.

Ears

Small, big, round, pointed – ears can say a lot, whether you are adding a comic, fantasy or realistic look.

A simple cone is the perfect nose for our festive Father Christmas (see page 67).

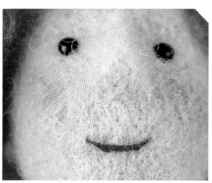

Just a few fibres needled into the face create a simple smile (see page 97).

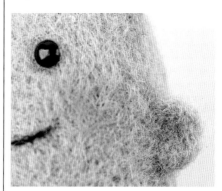

Danny Doodoll loves his simple little rounded ears (see page 69).

Our Christmas Fairy looks cute with her teeny button nose (see page 99).

Small sweetheart lips are ideal for cuter dolls (see page 107).

Mother Earth, life giver and the personification of nature, has pointed ears (see page 139).

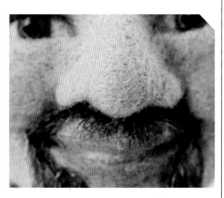

Adding shaped nostrils creates a more realistic look (see page 155).

Full lips with teeth are not as difficult as they look (see page 161).

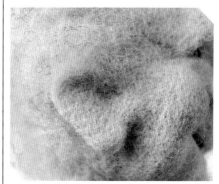

The Silver Surfer's ears are a prominent feature and have grown longer with age (see page 119).

Hair

There is so much fun to be had when you start playing with hair ideas and different styles. Learn from us, then look for unusual wools and colours, and let your imagination fly.

Kawaii Kate's fringe and ponytails are needle felted separately before they are attached to her head (see page 107).

Our Woolly Witch has conjured up dyed Wensleydale locks to complement her dress and hat (see page 153).

Daisy's colourful spiky hair enhances her comic look. Fibres are needle felted into mini cones which are then needled into her head (see page 75).

Facial hair

Facial hair can really enhance a face and give it character, whether you are adding bushy eyebrows, a stylish goatee or a full beard.

Knitting Nigel raises his fluffy eyebrows as he drops yet another stitch (see page 85).

Grey flyaway hair, fluffy eyebrows and a mini beard look good on our fun-loving old surfer (see page 119).

Curly Wensleydale locks give our king a jaunty hairstyle and moustache (see page 67).

Hair accessories

Finishing touches are so important. A knitted or needle-felted hat, a bow or just a plain hair band can enhance a character.

Nigel's warm and cosy hat reflects his love of knitting (see page 85).

A needle-felted hair band and a pretty bow are perfect for this little dancer (see page 83).

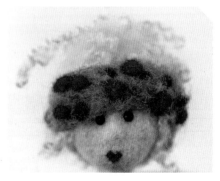

A seasonal wreath is just right for our Christmas Fairy (see page 99).

Hands

Our students often panic at the mention of hands! They are not difficult and even a simple mitten hand can be really effective.

Feet

In the projects we show how to needle felt bare feet as well as giving a range of ideas for shoes, boots and dainty slippers.

Clothes

Wool is incredibly versatile, offering multiple choices for needle-felted and wet-felted outfits. Clothes can either be needled straight on to the doll, or they can be made separately and then attached.

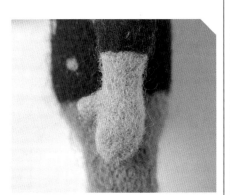

Danny Doodoll has cartoon-like mitten hands to complement his simple body shape (see page 69).

As with hands, needle felting feet and toes is easier than it looks (see page 119).

Loose wool and glitter fibres can be added to pretty dresses to create fluffy sleeves and hems (see page 105).

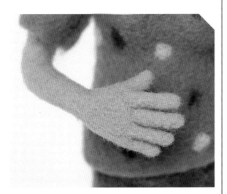

Making realistic hands is easier than it looks (see page 129).

These laced boots are made to match stylish striped stockings (see page 155).

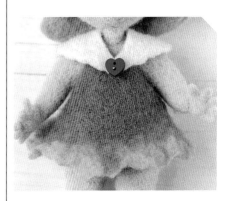

A wet-felted pink frilly dress with a needle-felted collar is perfect for Cute Caroline (see page 117).

Coloured wool has been used to make this glove which is edged with a fluffy cuff (see page 155).

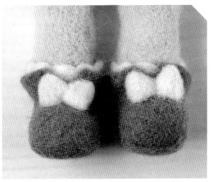

Sweet bootees embellished with bows are perfect for Cute Caroline (see page 117).

The colourful wet-felted shirt and shorts complement Gloria's needle-felted top (see page 127).

The PROJECTS

Order of working with needles

On larger shapes the order of working is generally as follows:

1. Three-needle tool – to control the fibres.

2. 40 triangle needle – to refine the shape.

3. Five-needle tool – to speed up the process.

4. 40 triangle needle – to tidy up the shape.

5. 40 twisted needle – to smooth the surface.

Roll the shape between your hands frequently throughout.

If you are working on smaller shapes, follow the instructions in the projects.

Important to remember

- Refer to the templates when measuring the shapes, remembering that the wool will shrink by approximately a third when needle felted (see page 29).
- Always work on the foam pad when needling.
- It is important to needle felt the shapes evenly. We find that it helps to work down them in lines.
- Take time to step back and check on the shape of your doll. Wool can be added at any point to balance or alter a figure.
- You will only achieve a smooth surface if the felting beneath is completely firm. Once needled smooth, you can trim flyaway fibres with curved embroidery scissors or work over larger shapes with a fuzz remover tool.

QUEEN OF HEARTS

. . . .

no armature * *simple shapes* * *using a cookie cutter*

Her mini Majesty is all dressed up and ready to go to our annual ball at Felty Towers. In this first project you will be building up simple shapes to make a doll. The combined head and body is a needle-felted cone to which a cone-shaped nose, sausage arms and teeny feet are added. No wire armature is used, so it is important to needle felt the shapes firmly. Queenie's heart-shaped handbag is created using a cookie cutter. The carefully selected extra accessories are precious royal treasures from our woolly vaults.

Finished size

• 17cm (6¾in)

What you need

• Templates for size and shape (see page 162)
• Foam pad
• Digital scales
• Coarse wool: approximately 16g (½oz) flesh-coloured, 10g (⅓oz) white, small amount of pink, small amount of white carded with a few glitter fibres
• Felting needles: 40 triangle, 40 twisted
• Three-needle tool
• Five-needle tool
• Barbeque stick
• Bradawl
• Strong clear glue

• Two 2mm (⅛in) round wire-backed glass eyes: black
• Curved embroidery scissors
• Craft knife
• Soft pastel: pink
• Small paintbrush
• Acid-free fixative
• Carders
• Miniature crown: gold
• String of mini pearls 8cm (3¼in)
• Heart-shaped cookie cutter
• Towel
• Gem: pink
• Sewing needle and thread

Head and body

1 Lay 15g (½oz) of flesh-coloured wool on the foam pad. To create a cone shape fold the left side into the middle to make it thicker.

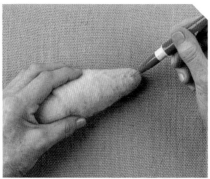

2 Roll the fibres tightly to expel the air. You will now have one thick end and one thin end. Using the three-needle tool, needle the thinner end to create the rounded head.

3 Continue working down the cone in this way. Every now and again, roll the cone firmly between your hands to even up the shape. Continue needling until smooth and firm.

4 Turn the cone, needle the bottom flat and then use the five-needle tool to firm it up before using the 40 triangle needle and then the twisted needle to finish and smooth.

5 Dress Needle a thin length of white coarse fibres around the cone to outline the neckline of the dress.

6 Lay fibres loosely over the body from the neckline down and use a 40 triangle needle to stab them into the cone. Cover it completely and then work over the dress with the twisted needle to neaten and smooth.

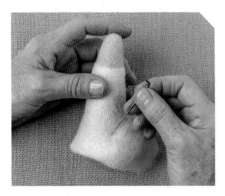

7 Wrap 2g (¹⁄₁₆oz) of white wool loosely around the base. Needle this into the dress with the 40 triangle needle to create a flared hem.

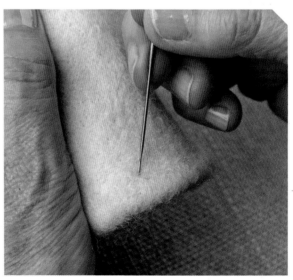

8 Needle a smooth join, then use the twisted needle to pin prick the surface with small stabs at a 45 degree angle to achieve a smooth, even finish and tuck away any flyaway fibres.

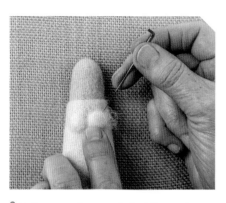

9 Using a small amount of white wool, roll two small, soft balls for breasts and needle them into the body below the neckline. Needle felt them until they are firm and smooth.

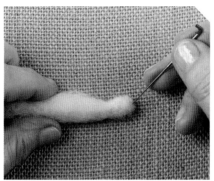

10 Arms Roll a small amount of white wool around a barbecue stick. Remove the stick and use the 40 triangle to needle felt a rounded end for the hand.

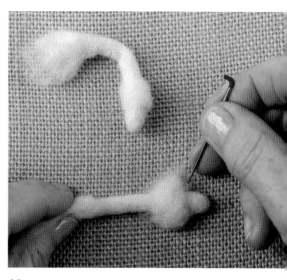

11 Needle felt the arms to match the template and bend one arm by needling into the bend to secure. Wrap wool fibres loosely around each wrist to create the fluffy cuff.

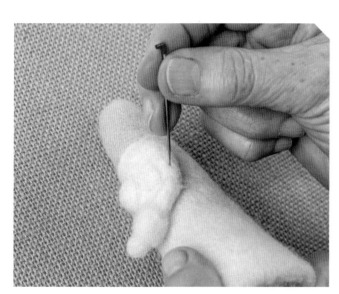

12 Splay out the loose fibres, press each arm into place and needle the fibres into the body to secure. Needle deeply into the upper part of the bent arm so that it lies firmly against the body.

13 Gently needle a length of white fibres around the neckline of the dress so that it remains fluffy but is secure.

Features

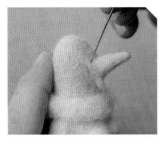

1 Nose Needle felt the small cone for the nose, press it onto the face and needle the loose fibres to secure. Use the 40 triangle needle to smooth the join.

2 Eyes Using a bradawl, make two eye holes above the nose. Next glue the eye wires and push the eyes into the head.

3 Mouth Lay a thin smile line of pink wool just under the nose and needle it into the face. Trim off any excess.

4 Cheeks Use a craft knife to scrape some pink pastel powder into a container. Gently brush this onto the cheeks.

Hair

1 Loosely place white wool, carded with glitter fibres, around the head. Gently needle the fibres in all round the face to secure them.

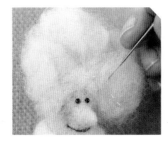

Finishing touches

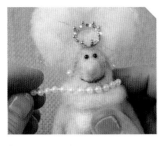

1 Glue the crown and the two pearl earrings onto the head and the pearl bead strip round the neck.

2 Needle felt two foot shapes and glue them to the base of the cone so that they peep out from under the hem of the dress.

3 Bag Place pink fibres into the cookie cutter. Needle them with the 40 triangle needle until they flatten. Gently turn the cutter over and repeat a few times until the heart is firm.

4 Remove the heart and needle around the edge to neaten and firm up.

5 Needle an 8cm (3¾in) thin length of fibres on your pad. Roll it in wet hands a few times to continue the felting and then roll along a towel to dry.

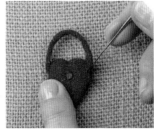

6 Glue a gem to the front of the heart then needle the strap to the bag.

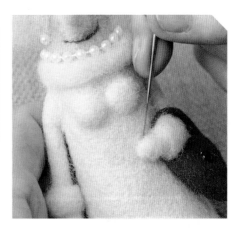

7 Slip the bag over the bent arm. Needle felt the hand into the body to secure the bag in place.

The king

The same template has been used to make a royal partner for the queen. A fun new character can be created with just a simple change of colour and hairstyle. He is 17cm (6¾in) tall.

Father Christmas

To make a bigger doll, just elongate the head, body and arm templates. Our festive Father Christmas has Wensleydale hair. The curly locks are needled into his head (see 'Finishing touches' – step 1 on page 104) before his beard and conical hat are added. The hat edging and bobble are lightly needle felted so they remain soft and fluffy. Father Christmas is 23cm (9in) tall.

DANNY DOODOLL

· ·

no armature * using an inner core * developing shapes

Danny Doodoll has just said goodbye to Daisy and Dylan (see page 75) and he is on his way to work with his new bag. This project introduces you to shaping simple limbs before they are attached to a body. Danny does not have an armature as his legs and feet are sturdy and firm enough to support his weight. His stylish hair style is created using rolled, softly felted cones which are needled straight into his head.

Finished size

• 18cm (7⅛in)

What you need

• Templates for size and shape (see page 162)
• Foam pad
• Digital scales
• Core wool: 20g (¾oz)
• Yarn
• Coarse wool: approximately 6g (⅕oz) beige, 5g (⅙oz) blue, 3g (⅒oz) black, 9g (³⁄₁₀oz) grey, 4g (⅐oz) rust
• Merino wool: small amount of black
• Felting needles: 40 triangle, 40 twisted
• Five-needle tool
• Three-needle tool
• Barbecue stick
• Curved embroidery scissors
• Bradawl
• Strong clear glue
• Two 4mm (¼in) wire-backed glass eyes: black
• Craft knife
• Soft pastel: red
• Small paintbrush
• Acid-free fixative
• Two small buttons: blue
• Towel

Head and body

1 Refer to the template and with 20g (¾oz) of core wool create a long knotted inner core. Wrap it tightly with yarn to secure it (see page 51).

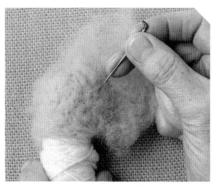

2 Use 2g (¹⁄₁₆oz) of beige wool to cover the top section. Needle deeply and evenly, using the 40 triangle needle, to attach the wool firmly.

3 Use the five-needle tool to speed up the process and then the 40 triangle and 40 twisted needles to finish and smooth the surface.

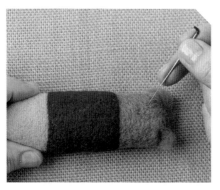

4 In the same way cover the next two sections in blue and grey wools and then needle the bottom of the body flat so that the legs can be attached easily.

5 Feet and legs Roll 3.5g (¹⁄₈oz) of grey wool into a thick sausage and needle felt the end round with the 40 triangle needle to create the foot shape.

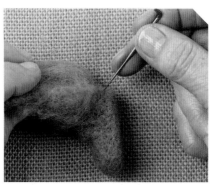

6 Needle felt the bottom of the foot flat. Continue to needle the foot until it matches the template for size and shape and then bend the fibres and needle into the bend to create the heel.

7 Continue needle felting the leg to match the template. Work over with the 40 twisted needle to smooth.

8 Outline the top of the boot with black wool. Fill in to cover. Make the other leg.

9 Splay out the loose fibres on one leg and press it onto the body, needling the fibres into the body to secure. Attach the other leg in the same way.

Tip

As you work, push the right leg up into the body so the two feet will stand flat and the legs are the same length. Fill in any unevenness with more wool to make a smooth join.

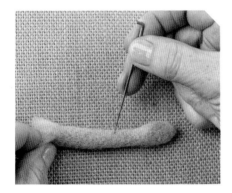

10 Arms Roll a small amount of beige wool around a barbecue stick. Remove the stick and needle felt the end into a leaf shape for the hand. Needle felt the fist of the arm, leaving loose fibres for attaching.

11 Needle felt a tiny sausage for the thumb.

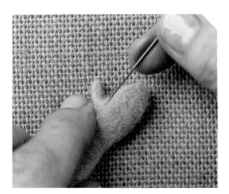

12 Splay out the loose thumb fibres, press it onto the hand and needle it to secure. Make the other arm in the same way.

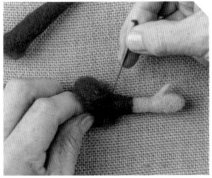

13 Needle felt blue wool over the arm using shallow stabs to prevent the beige wool fibres being pushed through to the other side. Leave loose fibres at the top.

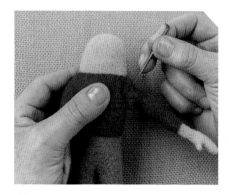

14 Attach the arms to the body and then use more blue wool to cover any visible beige.

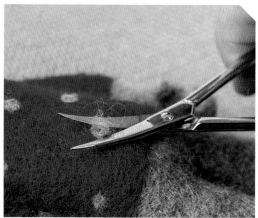

15 Needle small circles of grey wool onto the blue sweater and then use curved embroidery scissors to trim across each circle to neaten.

Features

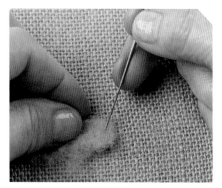

1 Ears Needle felt an ear shape on your pad, leaving loose fibres on one side for attaching.

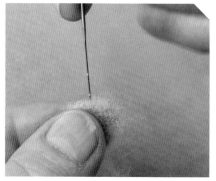

2 Needle around the rounded edges to neaten. Repeat for the other ear.

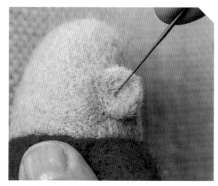

3 Splay out the fibres and attach the ears then needle deeply onto the centre of each ear to flatten them against the head.

4 Eyes Make eye holes with the bradawl. Glue the eye wires and insert the eyes.

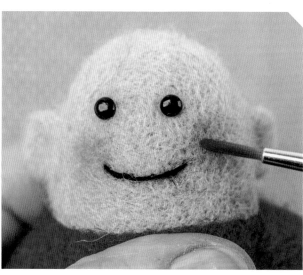

5 Needle a smile line using a wisp of black Merino wool and then gently brush the cheeks with pastel powder.

Hair

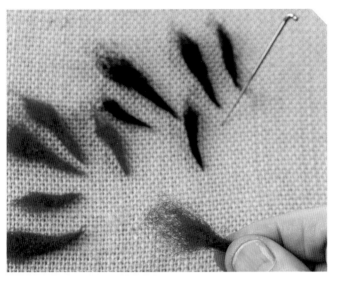

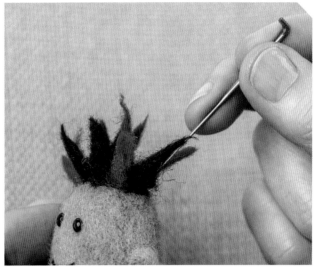

1 Needle felt small blue and black cones for the hair, rolling them between your fingers to speed up the process.

2 Needle all the cones onto the head, mixing the two colours.

Bag

1 Using rust-coloured wool, follow the steps on page 40 and the template on page 162 to needle felt a 1cm (½in) thick rectangle.

2 Referring to the template, needle felt the flap with the 40 triangle needle, leaving loose fibres along one side. Flip the flap now and again and continue needling to firm up, using the five-needle tool.

3 Once the shape has been neatened with a 40 twisted needle, work around the edge, gently tucking in any flyaway fibres.

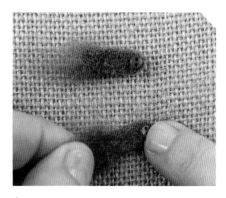

4 In the same way, needle felt two small straps and glue a button to each.

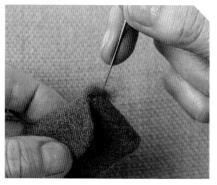

5 Attach the flap to the long edge of the bag on one side.

6 Attach the small straps to the flap.

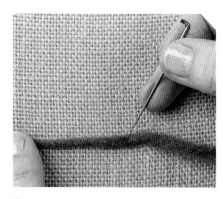

7 Shoulder strap Lay an 18cm (7⅛in) thin length of wool on your pad and gently needle until the fibres start to bind together (see page 40).

8 Roll the strip between wet hands, then roll on a towel to dry and finish the felting process.

9 Attach the strap to the bag and slip the finished bag over Danny's head.

Dylan

While Danny is busy at work, Dylan and his mum Daisy are off to the park. Dylan is three-quarters the size of his mum and dad. Just reduce the template size to 75 per cent to make him and your own woolly family.

Daisy

Daisy's body has the same inner core as Danny's with different colours chosen for her dress. Dainty purple shoes and a mini handbag (see template on page 162) complete her outfit.

LITTLE DANCER

. . . .

jointing * creative embellishments

Little Lotti loves to dance so we have jointed her body, which allows her arms and legs to move easily. Limbs should be needle felted firmly before they are jointed – this will prevent the jointing tape from loosening over time. Lotti's body shapes are small, so do take care and watch your fingers when felting with the sharp needles! She is wearing a mini skirt, which is a flat piece that is needle felted separately and then attached to the body. Delicate flower embellishments and a lace petticoat give her a pretty, dainty look.

Finished size

• 16cm (6¼in)

What you need

• Templates for size and shape (see page 163)
• Foam pad
• Digital scales
• Coarse wool: approximately 10g (⅓oz) flesh-coloured, 5g (⅙oz) dark pink, small amounts of green
• Merino wool: a little bright pink and pale pink
• Felting needles: 40 triangle, 38 triangle, 40 twisted
• Three-needle tool
• Five-needle tool
• Curved embroidery scissors
• Bradawl
• Strong clear glue
• Two 2mm (⅛in) wire-backed glass eyes: black
• Soft pastel: pink
• Craft knife
• Small paintbrush
• Acid-free fixative
• Wire: **neck** 6cm (2½in) length of 1.6mm (16 gauge)
• Wire cutters
• Steam iron
• Lace: **skirt** 25cm (9¾in), **hair ribbon** 6cm (2½in)
• Sewing needle and cotton for stitching
• Long sewing needle and dental tape for jointing
• Sari silk strands for hair

Head and body

1 Head Roll 2g (1/16oz) of wool into a tight ball and use a 40 triangle needle to needle felt it until it is firm. Use the twisted needle to smooth the surface.

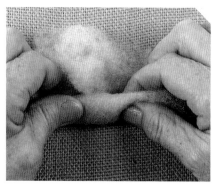

2 Body Lay 3g (1/10oz) of wool on the pad, fold the left side in and then roll it into a tight sausage.

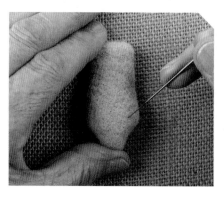

3 Needle felt the body using the three-needle tool and then the 40 triangle needle until it is firm and matches the template for size and shape.

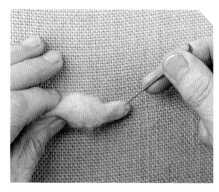

4 Arms Roll a small amount of wool around a barbecue stick into a tight sausage for one arm. Remove the stick and needle the end of the sausage into a leaf shape for the hand using a 40 triangle needle.

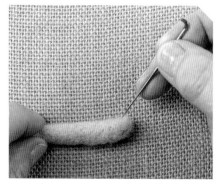

5 Referring to the template, continue needle felting the arm, rolling it between your palms occasionally to speed up the process. Flatten the top inside area so that it will lie snugly against the body.

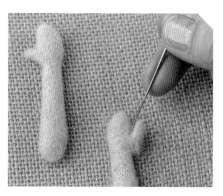

6 Needle felt a tiny sausage for the thumb using the 40 triangle needle and attach it to the hand. Repeat for the other arm.

7 Legs Referring to the template, roll a 2g (1/16oz) tight sausage around the stick for one leg and needle felt up to the knee. Bend the wool at the knee and needle into the bend.

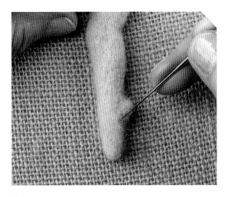

8 Flatten the top of the leg slightly so that it will lay snuggly against the body. Needle felt a small ball and attach it to the back of the leg for the heel.

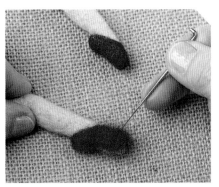

9 Cover the foot with red wool and needle it smooth to create the ballet shoe. Repeat for the other leg.

Features

1 Nose Using the 40 triangle needle, needle the end of a few fibres until firm, then splay out the loose fibres. Press the nose onto the face and gently needle in the loose fibres.

2 Eyes Make two eye holes with a bradawl, glue the wire eyes and push them into the holes.

3 Mouth Using bright pink Merino wool, first needle a smile line. Needle two small triangles above it to create the top lip.

4 Needle a small semi-circle below the line. Trim off any wisps of excess wool.

5 Brush the cheeks with a little pastel powder.

Attaching the head

1 Use a bradawl to make a hole up into the bottom of the head and down into the neck. Glue the ends of a 6cm (2½in) length of wire and push the head onto one end and the body onto the other, leaving 1cm (½in) showing for the neck.

2 Using the 38 triangle needle, wrap the neck wire loosely with wool and needle it smoothly into the head and the body to secure.

Tips

We advise using a thicker 38 triangle needle when working near wire.

To avoid pricking your fingers, you can sandwich the edge of the skirt between a piece of folded card and then neaten with the needle.

Woolly wardrobe

1 Dress Cover the top of the body with dark pink wool and use the twisted needle to smooth.

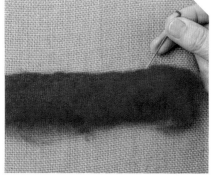

2 Skirt Lay out a 20 x 3.5cm (8 x 1¼in) strip of dark pink wool on the pad. Turn the top fibres in and, with the 40 triangle needle, needle to neaten the top edge. Leave loose fibres along the lower edge and sides.

3 Needle the strip with the five-needle tool, flipping it frequently until it is firm, then neaten the top edge. Iron with a steam iron, leaving the loose fibres.

4 Flower decorations Use the 40 triangle needle to needle a wisp of pale pink Merino wool into the strip, then pull the outer flyaway fibres into the middle with the tip of your needle and stab. Repeat this process all round until the shape looks like a mini doughnut. Cover the strip.

5 Add one flower to the bodice neckline. Add a few green fibres to one side of each pink flower, for a leaf.

6 Wrap the skirt loosely around the body. Gather slightly and needle the loose fibres into the waist to give a smooth join.

7 Gently needle the two ends together to complete the skirt.

9 Sew up the back join.

8 Sew along the top of the lace with a running stitch. Gather and fit around the hips just under the skirt and tie to secure.

Jointing

We use durable dental tape to joint our dolls and the jointing method is the same for the arms and legs. Your needle should be long enough to go through one limb, the body and the second limb, with enough of the needle protruding so that you can hold it.

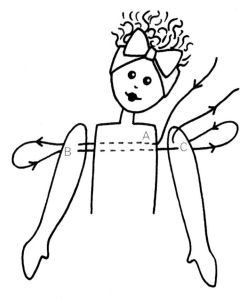

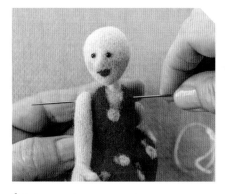

1 Following the diagram, thread 40cm (15¾in) of dental tape through the doll's body at point A, leaving a 10cm (4in) tail. Pass the needle through the top of her right arm.

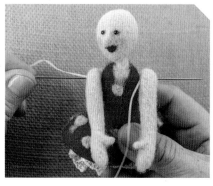

2 Thread the needle back through the arm at point B and then back through the body and the second arm.

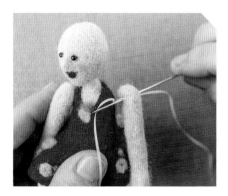

3 Pass the needle back through the arm at point C.

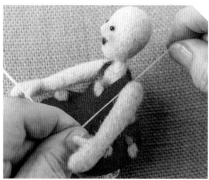

4 Pull the tape tightly and tie the ends together in a double knot.

5 Thread the ends of the tape, one by one, through the back of the body and trim. Needle a few fibres in to cover any indentations caused by the tape. Repeat for the legs.

Needle felt all the limbs firmly so that the jointing tape does not loosen over time.

Hair

1 Needle some silk strands to the back and top of the head.

2 Wrap the head with a thin strip of dark pink wool, needling it into the top of the head to secure.

3 Tie a knot in the middle of the hair ribbon lace, trim the ends to create a bow and glue it to the head.

Mixing and matching colours is fun so why not create a mini dancing troupe to entertain your other dolls and woolly characters. To make Lily – our turquoise dancer – we enlarged the template by 30 per cent. Experiment and enjoy.

KNITTING NIGEL

· ·

*no armature * telling a story * creating character*

Nigel was born out of loving memories of our Nanny Flo who adored knitting and created new sweaters for us at the drop of a hat! Nigel is not so deft and has dropped quite a few stitches since he learnt how to knit. He likes nothing more than spending an evening knitting and nattering with friends at his local village hall.

As he is seated, Nigel's legs do not have to support his weight so an armature is not needed. His chair is sculpted from foam before being needle felted with wool and this is made first so that Nigel can snuggle into it comfortably. We have provided patterns – woolly knits – and instructions for all his clothes and accessories, so search your crafty cupboards for some brightly coloured wools. You will only need small amounts of yarn for his mini wardrobe.

Finished size

• 26cm (10¼in) tall – seated without the chair

What you need

CHAIR
• High density foam pieces (L x H x D):
three 12 x 9 x 4cm (4¾ x 3½ x 1½in),
one 9 x 9 x 4cm (3½ x 3½ x 1½in)
• Ballpoint pen
• Craft knife
• Large scissors
• Digital scales
• Coarse wool: 10g (⅓oz) bright turquoise and
2g (¹⁄₁₆oz) pale turquoise
• Felting needles: 40 triangle, 40 twisted
• Five-needle tool
• Embroidery scissors
• Felt tip pen: dark blue
• Glue gun
• Polymer clay: brown

KNITTING PATTERNS
• Knitting needles: size 4 (US 10)
• Socks and knitting bag yarn: 4-ply, cream
• Tank top, hat and Nigel's knitting project:
4-ply, multi-coloured
• Cushion and rug yarn: double knitting pale blue
• Tapestry needle
• Small amount of wadding (batting) to
stuff cushion

NIGEL
• Templates for size and shape (see page 164)
• Foam pad
• Digital scales
• Coarse wool: approximately 45g (1½oz)
flesh-coloured, 4g (⅛oz) dark brown, small amount
of black, 5g (⅙oz) white, small amounts of carded
light brown and rust for hair

- Felting needles: 40 triangle, 38 triangle, three-needle tool, five-needle tool
- Bradawl
- Strong clear glue
- Two 2mm (⅛in) wire-backed glass eyes: black
- Soft pastel: red
- Craft knife
- Small paintbrush
- Acid-free fixative
- One barbecue stick for making arms and legs
- Darning needle and yarn for laces
- Wire: **neck** 8cm (3¼in) length 1.6mm (16 gauge)
- Wire cutters
- Two barbecue sticks for mini knitting needles
- Small amount of polymer clay
- Acrylic paint: grey
- Curved embroidery scissors

Making the chair

This is an easy and inexpensive way to create a comfortable chair. Foam blocks are trimmed to shape before wool fibres are needled into them, then they are glued together. To create the chair, stack the foam shapes as shown in diagram 1.

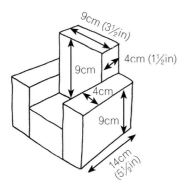

Diagram 1
Foam shapes assembled.

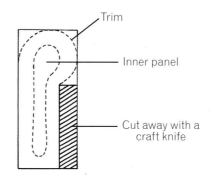

Diagram 2
To create a rounded arm, first cut the shaded rectangle away using a craft knife, before trimming with scissors.

Diagram 3
Trimmed foam shapes ready for needle felting.

1 Referring to diagram 2, draw the shape of the arms onto the ends of the two 14 x 9cm (5½ x 3½in) pieces of foam.

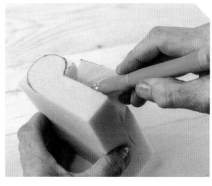

2 Use a craft knife to cut the strip away under the arm.

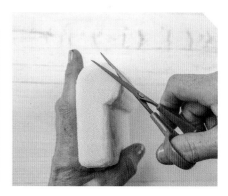

3 Use scissors to trim away the edges to create the rounded look.

4 Round off the edges of the remaining foam pieces (see diagram 3).

5 Lay wool over the foam shapes and needle felt it into the foam to secure the fibres.

6 Work over the surfaces first with the five-needle tool and then with the 40 triangle and twisted needles to firm up and smooth.

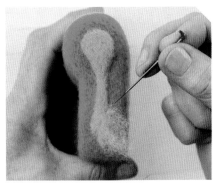

7 Using pale turquoise wool, needle felt the inner panel onto the front of the arms (see diagram 2).

8 Use a dark blue pen to draw evenly spaced spots over all the wool covered shapes and then glue the shapes together to create the armchair.

9 Roll four 2cm (¾in) diameter and four 1cm (½in) diameter balls of polymer clay. Press the smaller balls on top of the larger ones and bake according to the manufacturer's instructions.

10 When baked use the glue gun to attach one to each corner of the chair base for casters.

Knitting patterns

As Nigel will need his socks and tank top before you finish needle felting his body, it is a good idea to knit these first.

Sock tops

Cast on 12 sts.
Knit every row until your knitting measures 2.5cm (1in).
Cast (bind) off. Sew up the side seam to create a tube.
Repeat.

Tank top

You can also use this pattern to knit Patchwork Pam's dress (see page 97).

Front
Cast on 16 sts.
Knit 24 rows (knit 56 rows for Patchwork Pam's dress, then continue as below).
Cast off 2 sts at the beginning of the next 2 rows.
K6, turn and continue knitting on these stitches as follows:
*K1, K2tog, K3.
Knit 3 rows.
K1, K2tog, K2.
Knit 3 rows.
K1, K2tog, K1 (3 sts remaining).
Knit 3 rows.
Cast (bind) off.*
Continue on remaining 6 sts as follows:
Repeat from * to *.

Back
Cast on 16 sts.
Knit 24 rows.
Cast (bind) off 2 sts at the beginning of the next 2 rows (12 sts).
Knit 12 rows.
Cast (bind) off.

Making up
Sew in ends to neaten then sew one side and shoulder seam. The remaining side and shoulder seam will be sewn once the top is fitted onto the body.

It's time to create some woolly knits for Nigel to keep him warm while he sits knitting his own project.

Head

As Nigel does not have an armature, all the needle-felted shapes should be very firm so that he can maintain his pose.

1 Tightly roll and then needle felt a 5g (1/6oz) ball of wool with a 40 triangle needle until it is firm and matches the template. Work over the surface with the twisted needle to smooth.

2 Using a 40 triangle needle, needle felt the middle of 2g (1/16oz) fibres to create a soft pad. Press it onto the back of the head and needle to attach.

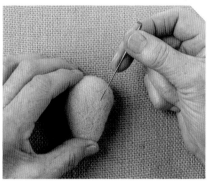

3 Work over the head with the 40 twisted needle to smooth the surface.

Features

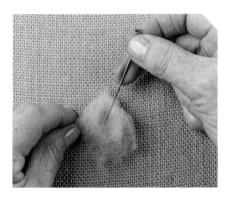

1 Nose Use a 40 triangle needle to needle into the middle of a small bundle of fibres to firm them up.

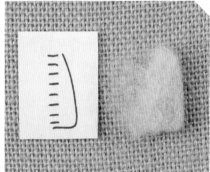

2 Fold the pad in half and needle into the fold to firm it up and create the bridge of the nose. Needle into the bottom of the nose to sculpt it.

3 Unfold the nose and splay out the fibres. Press it onto the face and needle the loose fibres to create a smooth join. Needle repeatedly into the eye areas for the eye sockets.

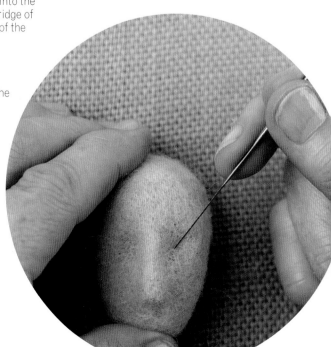

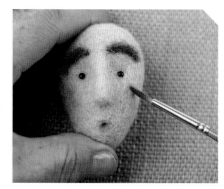

4 Eyes Use the bradawl to create holes for the eyes. Glue the eye wires and push them into the holes.

5 Gently needle two brown wool fluffy eyebrows. Trim off any excess.

6 Make a hole for the mouth with the bradawl and then colour round the hole and the cheeks with pastel powder.

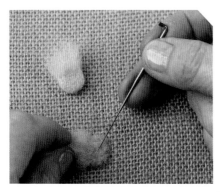

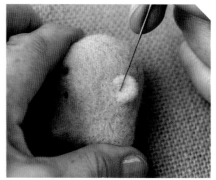

7 Ears Refer to the template and needle felt two small semi-circles.

8 Attach the ears and then needle into the middle of them to flatten them against the head.

Tip

Here you are working with a larger amount of wool. Make sure you roll it tightly and hold the wool securely as you needle felt, otherwise the fibres will spring out and the needle felting process will take longer.

Body

1 Lay 14g (½oz) of flesh-coloured coarse wool on the pad. Fold one end in to thicken and then roll it into a tight sausage.

2 Use the three-needle tool to needle felt the thin end until it starts to firm up and matches the template.

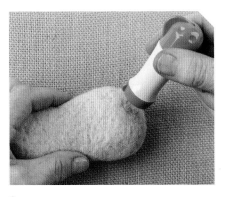

3 Turn the shape round and needle the thicker end. Once it is firm and round, you can use the five-needle tool to speed up the felting.

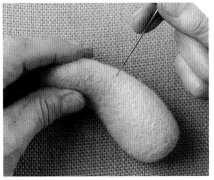

4 Finish working over the body with a 40 triangle then a 40 twisted needle to smooth and refine the shape. Bend the body slightly and needle into the bend to give a slumped look.

Tip

If you want to give Nigel a little more shape, this is the time to do it. Using the 40 triangle needle lightly needle felt a 2g (¹⁄₁₆oz) pad of wool and attach it to his tummy or bottom – or both.

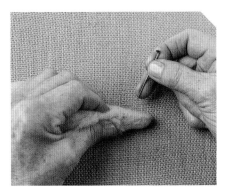

5 Legs Roll 8g (¼oz) of wool into a tight sausage around a barbecue stick. Remove the stick and needle the end until firm to create the foot. Needle the bottom of the foot flat.

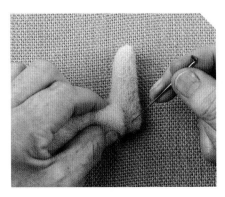

6 Keeping the top rounded, the bottom flat and referring to the template, needle felt until the foot measures 4cm (1½in) then bend the wool up to create the heel and needle to secure.

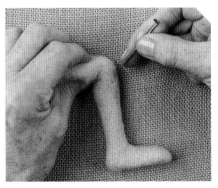

7 Needle felt the ankle, packing the wool down into the sausage to firm and build it up until you reach the knee. Bend the wool sausage again to create the knee and needle this area until firm.

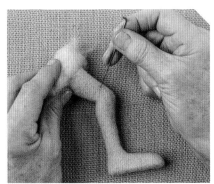

8 Continue needle felting the upper leg and thigh, adding more wool to thicken this area if necessary. Work over the leg with the 40 twisted needle to smooth. Leave loose ends for attaching. Make two legs.

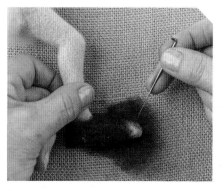

9 Boots Needle felt dark brown wool into the foot to create the boot.

10 Using black wool needle felt a heel and sole to the bottom of the boot.

11 Referring to the template, needle felt a boot tongue and attach it to the top of the boot.

12 Slide a knitted sock top over the foot onto the ankle so that it lies behind the tongue.

13 Referring to the template and instructions on page 42, needle felt two boot collars. Wrap one round each ankle and needle the loose fibres into each foot to secure.

14 Sew yarn laces into each boot and tie them in a bow (see diagram).

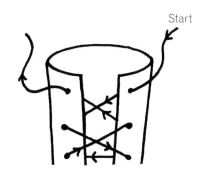

Start

Lacing boots

Following the arrows, and starting at the top right, sew the laces through the boot collar.

15 Press the legs onto the body and needle felt the loose fibres until they are secure and firm. You may need to add more wool to fill in any holes or soft areas and to make sure the legs are firmly attached.

16 Make sure that Nigel can sit comfortably! Make adjustments to his leg positioning if necessary.

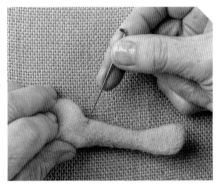

17 Arms Roll 3.5g (⅛oz) wool round a barbecue stick. Remove the stick and needle felt the hand and the lower arm using the template to help you.

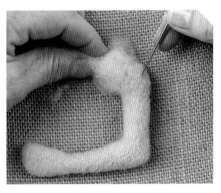

18 Bend the wool when you reach the elbow, checking that the hand will lie in the right direction for the pose. Continue needle felting the wool up to the shoulder adding more wool if necessary.

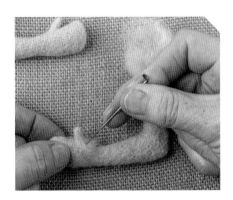

19 Needle felt the thumb and attach it to the hand. Make two arms.

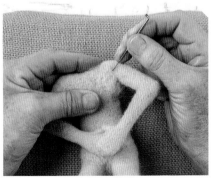

20 Press the arms into place so that they stand away from the body and needle the loose fibres to secure. Make sure the join is very firm, adding more wool to the underarm area to keep the arms raised if necessary.

Tip

It is easier to ensure that the two arms are the same size if you measure the second against the finished one as you work.

Attaching the head

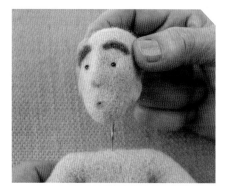

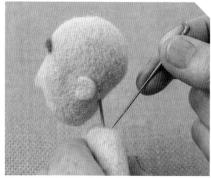

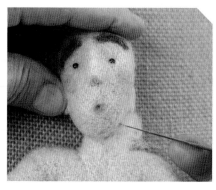

1 Use the bradawl to make a 5cm (2in) deep hole in the top of the body and a 2cm (¾in) deep hole up into the head. Glue the ends of the neck wire and push it into the body. Push the head onto the other end, leaving a gap for the neck.

2 Using the 38 triangle needle, carefully needle the wool around the ends of the wire. This causes the wool to shrink and tighten.

3 Once the glue has set hard, wrap the neck wire loosely with wool. Use a 38 triangle needle to needle the wool up into the head and down into the body. Create a smooth join from the head to the shoulders.

Woolly wardrobe

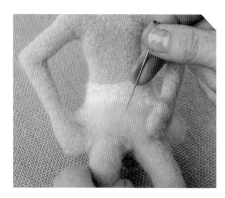

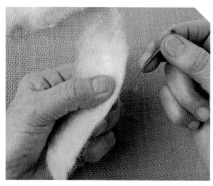

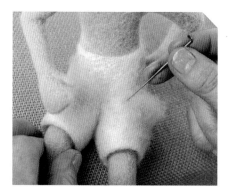

1 Shorts Needle white wool from the waist down to cover Nigel's tummy and bottom.

2 Referring to the template for size and shape, and following the steps on page 42, needle felt the two flat strips for the shorts, a small amount of white wool for each.

3 Wrap the strips around the tops of the legs and needle the loose fibres into the body so that there is a smooth join. The shorts fit loosely on Nigel's legs, making them look reaslistic.

Finishing touches

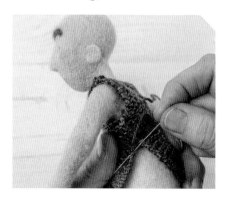

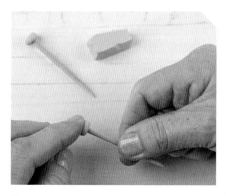

1 Slip the tank top onto Nigel and sew up the shoulder and side seams.

2 Arrange the carded wool on the head. Needle in to create the hairstyle, but keep it fluffy.

3 Knitting needles Using the pointed ends cut two barbecue sticks measuring 7cm (2¾in). Roll two small balls of polymer clay and press them onto the sticks. Bake according to the manufacturer's instructions.

Tip
Use the 40 twisted needle to work over all the visible flesh areas to smooth the surface. It can then be trimmed to remove any final flyaway fibres.

4 Paint the mini knitting needles grey. When dry, transfer Nigel's knitting onto the needles, dropping a few stitches along the way to tell his story.

5 Sit Nigel in his chair and glue the needles to his hands.

6 Roll some of the remaining wool into a small ball so that it trails down to the floor. Pop Nigel's hat on and the cosy rug in front of the chair. Add the knitted cushion, then fill Nigel's knitting bag with small balls of wool and maybe an extra hat or two.

Knitting patterns

You have made some clothes for Nigel, now it's time for some more woolly knits.

Hat

Cast on 30 sts and work 2 rows in rib (knit 1, purl 1).
Work next two rows in stocking (stockinette) stitch, starting with a knit row then a purl row.
Continue in stocking (stockinette) stitch, decreasing on the knit rows as follows:

Row 1: K4, K2tog, K8, K2tog, K8, K2tog, K4 (27 sts).
Row 3: K4, K2tog, K7, K2tog, K7, K2tog, K3 (24 sts).
Row 5: K4, K2tog, K6, K2tog, K6, K2tog, K2 (21 sts).
Row 7: K4, K2tog, K5, K2tog, K5, K2tog, K1 (18 sts).
Row 9: K4, K2tog K4, K2tog, K4, K2tog (15 sts).
Row 11: K4, K2tog, K3, K2tog, K3 (12 sts).
Cut the yarn to a 30cm (11¾in) length. Thread it onto a needle and through the remaining 12 stitches. Pull tight.

Making up
With right sides together, sew the hat seam together. Work the remaining end in neatly.

Nigel's knitting

Cast on 10 sts and knit 24 rows.

Cushion

Cast on 18 sts and knit in stocking (stockinette) stitch – 1 row knit then 1 row purl, until you have knitted a square. Cast (bind) off. Make two squares.

Making up
Place right sides together, sew up three seams then turn the cushion to the right side. Add a little wadding and sew up the final seam.

Knitting bag

Cast on 16 sts.
Knit every row until it measures 8cm (3¼in).
Cast (bind) off.
Finger knit two 6cm (2½in) lengths for the handles.

Making up
Fold the knitting in half and sew the two side seams together. Turn the bag and sew one handle to each side.

Rug

Cast on 40 sts and knit for 10cm (4in).
Cast (bind) off.

Pam loves nothing better than a cosy evening in with her fiancé Nigel. She is busy knitting a colourful patchwork blanket ready for those cold winter months. Use Nigel's templates to needle felt Pam's body, adding breasts as described on page 38. Her dress is a longer version of Nigel's tank top and you can complement her wardrobe and hair with a matching armchair and colourful knitted props.

CHRISTMAS FAIRY

partial armature * working around wire * using glitter fibres

We love Christmas and it would not be the same without a beautiful festive fairy to delight us with her sparkly magic. A partial wire armature is used for her neck, arms and legs, which allows daintier limbs and easy posing. To help her stand on her own two feet she has big comfortable slippers. Teeny Wensleydale curls are used for her hair and fluffy loose fibres are carded with glitter fibres to edge her festive frock.

Finished size

• 22cm (8⅝in)

What you need

- Templates for size and shape (see page 165)
- Foam pad
- Digital scales
- Coarse wool: approximately 10g (⅓oz) flesh-coloured, 13g (⁷⁄₁₆oz) white, small amounts of green and red
- Merino wool: small amount of red, 5g (⅙oz) flesh-coloured to match coarse wool
- Wensleydale wool: small amount for hair
- Glitter fibres: small amount of pink
- Felting needles: 40 triangle, 38 triangle, 40 twisted
- Three-needle tool
- Curved embroidery scissors
- Bradawl
- Strong clear glue

- Two 3mm (⅛in) wire-backed glass eyes: black
- Soft pastel: red
- Craft knife
- Small paintbrush
- Acid-free fixative
- Wire: **arms** 18cm (7⅛in) length of 1mm (18 gauge), **legs** 30cm (11¾in) length of 1.6mm (16 gauge), **neck** 6cm (2½in) length of 1.6mm (16 gauge), **wings** 28cm (11in) length of 0.7mm (22 gauge)
- Wire cutters
- Round-nosed pliers
- Carders
- Knitting needle
- Miniature basket
- Acrylic paint: white
- Large star sequin: silver

Woolly reminder

• Don't forget to change to a 38 triangle needle when working near wire.

Head

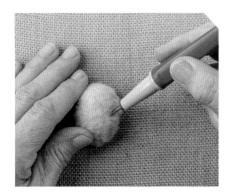

1 Refer to the templates for size and shape. Use 3g (1/10oz) of wool to needle felt the head with the three-needle tool.

2 Change to the 40 triangle needle to neaten and flatten one side of the head for the face.

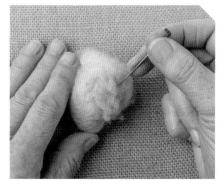

3 Needle felt the centre of a small amount of wool on the pad until it is semi-firm, then attach it to the back of the head to create the skull shape.

Features

4 Needle and shape with the 40 triangle needle and then work over the surface with the 40 twisted needle until it is smooth.

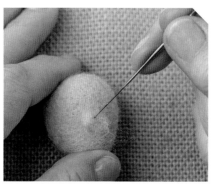

1 Nose Needle felt a few flesh-coloured fibres into a tiny ball on the pad with the 40 triangle needle. Attach it to the face and needle it to smooth the join.

2 Eyes Needle either side of the nose repeatedly to create the eye sockets. Make the eye holes with the bradawl and insert the glued eyes.

3 Mouth Needle a wisp of red Merino wool for the mouth. Add a few fibres above and below the line for the heart-shaped lips.

4 Brush over the cheeks with some pastel powder (see page 55).

Body

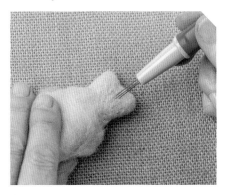

1 Lay 5g (⅙oz) of wool on your pad, fold the left side in to thicken and roll into a tight sausage. Needle the right side to create the shoulders with the three-needle tool.

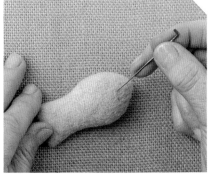

2 Turn it round and needle the other end to match the lower body. Needle until firm.

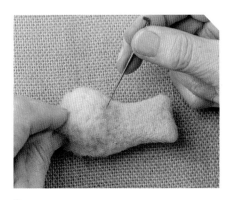

3 Needle felt another soft pad with a small amount of wool, using the three-needle tool and attach it to the back of the body to build up the bottom. Needle with the 40 triangle and then the 40 twisted needle to create a smooth join and finish.

4 Arms Use a bradawl to make a hole through the shoulders and then glue the centre of an 18cm (7⅛in) length of wire and thread it through the hole.

Tip

You can enlarge the bradawl hole with a knitting needle if the wire does not go through it easily.

5 Use the 38 triangle needle to attach the end of a thin length of flesh-coloured Merino wool to the body to secure. Smear the arm wire lightly with glue, then wrap the wool tightly down the wire to the end.

6 Fold the wire end over to trap the wool and create the hand.

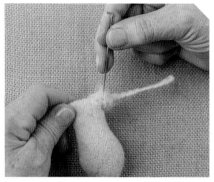

7 Smear the arm with a little glue and then wrap the wool back up the wire to the shoulder. Add a loose wrap of wool to the shoulder and needle to neaten with the 38 triangle needle. Repeat for the other arm.

8 Legs Glue the centre 3cm (1⅛in) of the thicker 30cm (11¾oz) leg wire, make a hole through the lower body and thread the wire through.

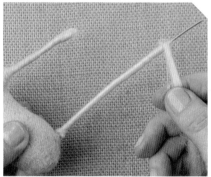

9 Wrap the glued legs with wool down to 3cm (1⅛in) from the end.

Leg wire

Lower body

2cm (¾in)

11cm (4⅜in)

11cm (4⅜in)

3cm (1⅛in)

Bend the wrapped legs down, then bend the feet wires before wrapping them with wool.

10 Bend the legs down and bend the last 3cm (1⅛in) wire ends to create the feet as shown in the diagram. Wrap more wool around the upper legs and needle for a smooth join into the body.

11 Needle felt two slippers firmly with the 40 triangle needle using 2g (¹⁄₁₆oz) of wool for each one. Make sure the bottoms are needled flat so that your fairy can stand.

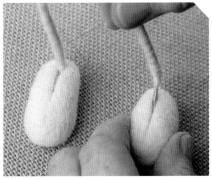

12 Make a slit in the top of each slipper with a craft knife and push a glued foot wire into each slit.

13 Needle a little wool over each slit to secure and neaten and then needle felt a small ball for each slipper bobble and glue them into place.

Attaching the head

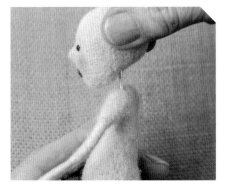

1 Make a hole in the head and one in the top of the body. Glue and insert one end of a 6cm (2½in) length of wire into the body and one end into the head, leaving a 1cm (½in) length showing for the neck.

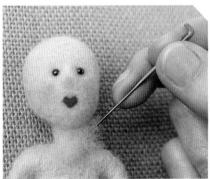

2 Wrap the wire loosely with wool and use the 38 triangle needle to needle gently up into the head and down into the body, to firm up and smooth the joins.

Woolly wardrobe

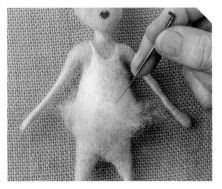

1 Dress Outline and then fill in the bodice of the dress with white wool.

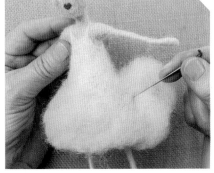

2 Card a few sparkly fibres into white wool and needle fibres around the hips so that they are soft and fluffy.

Wings

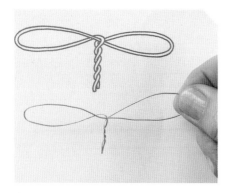

1 Refer to the template on page 165 and bend the 28cm (11in) wing wire. Wrap the trailing ends over the crossed wires, then twist them together.

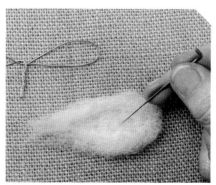

2 Place a layer of white wool on the pad, slightly larger than one wing, and needle felt the middle until flat using the 40 triangle needle tool to firm it up.

3 Lay one wire wing on top and fold the fibres up and over into the middle of the wing. Needle to secure using the 38 triangle needle.

4 Cover both wings in this way and then make a hole in the fairy's back. Glue the twisted wires and push them into the hole. Needle a few fibres over the join to neaten.

Finishing touches

1 Using a 40 triangle needle, gently needle a length of green wool around the head and then needle Wensleydale curls into place to create her hairstyle.

2 Decorate the headdress with small red needle-felted balls.

3 Paint the mini basket white and then pack it with green fibres and teeny red balls before hanging it over her arm. Glue a sequin star to her hand.

Twinkle Fairy

Adding some pink glittery fibres to this fairy's dress and hair makes her sparkle and shine. The glimmering gold crown and basket are perfect finishing touches.

Forest Fairy

Russet brown and leaf green wools have been used to create a sweet nature-loving fairy. Her hair is loosely needle felted to create a flyaway look and her slippers are decorated with woolly berries.

KAWAII KATE

. . . .

partial armature ∗ needle-felted eyes ∗ wet felting

'Kawaii' is the Japanese word for 'cute' and this culture is hugely popular in Japan and internationally. Known and much loved, it celebrates all that is positive and takes many forms in all aspects of the lifestyles of Japanese people. The dolls usually have large heads with big eyes and features portrayed lower on the face – which gives an endearing baby look. Quite often pastel colours are used and girl outfits are embellished with frills and bows. Kate is pretty in purple with her frilled wet-felted skirt, scalloped collar and matching socks. In this project we introduce you to a partial armature, more complex eyes and hands, and she has a needle-felted hairstyle with pretty bows. We have also included instructions for Bobbin, Kate's pet rabbit.

Finished size

• 23cm (9in)

What you need

KATE
• Templates for size and shape
(see pages 166–167)
• Foam pad
• Digital scales
• Core wool 25g ($\frac{7}{8}$oz)
• Yarn
• Coarse wool: approximately 43g
($1\frac{1}{2}$oz) brown, 4g ($\frac{1}{7}$oz) white, 15g
($\frac{1}{2}$oz) lavender, small amount of red
• Merino wool: small amounts
of orange, dark brown, white,
black, red
• Felting needles: 40 triangle,
38 triangle, 40 twisted
• Three-needle tool

• Five-needle tool
• Curved embroidery scissors
• Felt tip pen: black
• Soft pastel: pink
• Craft knife
• Small paintbrush
• Acid-free fixative
• Bradawl
• Knitting needle
• Strong clear glue
• Wire: **arms** 16cm ($6\frac{1}{4}$in) length of
1mm (18 gauge), **neck** 7cm ($2\frac{3}{4}$in)
length of 1.6mm (16 gauge)
• Wire cutters
• Steam iron
• Heart-shaped button: red

WET-FELTED SKIRT
• Coarse wool: 2g ($\frac{1}{16}$oz) lavender
• Merino wool: 2g ($\frac{1}{16}$oz) lavender
• Old towel
• Bubble wrap
• Netting
• Olive soap
• Grater
• Felting bulb spray, water sprinkler,
or old plastic bottle with holes
• Wet felting tool
• Scissors
• Rolling pin or a length of
pipe insulation
• Bowl

RABBIT

- Templates (see page 167)
- Coarse wool: 7g (¼oz) lavender
- Merino wool: a little black and pink
- Two 5mm (¼in) wire-backed glass eyes: black
- Pastel powder: pink
- Acid-free fixative
- 25cm (9¾in) ribbon: lavender

Woolly reminders

- Remember to use a 38 triangle needle when working near wire.
- There are more detailed instructions on making a round core on page 50.

Head

1 Roll 12g (²/₅oz) of core wool into a tight ball and wrap it tightly with yarn to secure (see page 50). The core ball should be flattened slightly and match the dotted line on the template.

2 Cover the ball loosely with brown wool and needle felt it in using the 40 triangle needle and then the five-needle tool to speed up the felting. Finally work over the ball with the twisted needle to smooth.

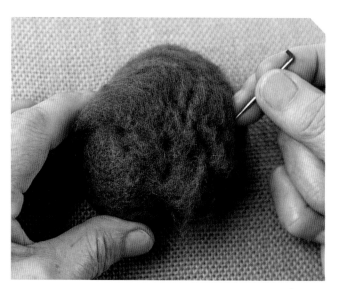

3 Needle felt a soft 4g (¹/₇oz) pad of wool and attach it to the back of the head to create the skull shape.

4 Work over the head to smooth and firm up, using the twisted needle.

Features

1 Cheeks, chin and nose Using the 40 triangle needle, needle felt the chin and cheeks shape and attach it to the lower face. Needle felt a small ball for the nose and attach it above the chin. Needle with the twisted needle to ensure smooth joins.

2 Eyes Referring to the template, mark the eye shapes with a felt tip pen.

3 Using the 40 triangle needle, repeatedly needle these areas until they are flat then needle white wool fibres into them.

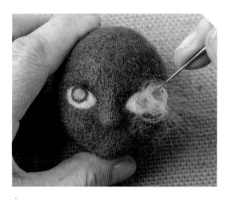

4 Using Merino wool, needle an orange circle for the iris and then outline it and shade the upper part of the circle with dark brown Merino wool.

5 Needle the black pupil and then add a white spot with a few white fibres.

6 Outline the eye shape with black Merino wool, thickening the upper lash line slightly. Add a few black lines for the outer lashes.

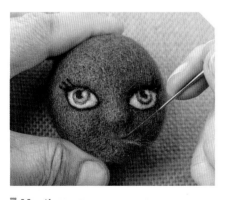

7 Mouth Needle a small smile line using red Merino wool. Needle two triangles above the line and a semi-circle below.

8 Ears Referring to the template for size and shape, needle felt two small semi-circles on the pad.

9 Splay out the loose fibres and press one onto each side of the head. Needle the loose fibres into the head to secure before needling into the centre of each ear to flatten them.

10 Gently brush pink pastel powder around the eyes, cheeks and chin (see page 55).

Hair

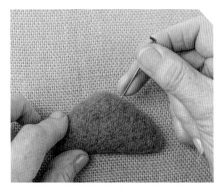

1 For the fringe, form a triangle with 2g (1/16 oz) of lavender wool on the pad. Gently needle felt the triangular shape with a 40 triangle needle, so it remains soft.

2 Place the fringe on the doll's head and needle felt the shape until it is firm and has shrunk to fit the head.

3 Cover the back and top of the head with more lavender wool and then needle a thin line of brown wool down the centre for the parting.

4 Needle felt two ponytails using the template for size and shape and attach one to each side of the head.

5 Roll a small amount of wool into a sausage. Needle one end into a triangle. Twist and needle the centre of the wool before needling a second triangle to create the bow.

6 Wrap the ponytail join with a thin length of wool, needle to secure then glue a bow to each ponytail.

Body

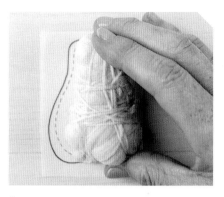

1 Use 13g (⅞₁₆oz) of core wool to create a pear-shaped long inner core (see page 51). Match this core to the dotted line on the template.

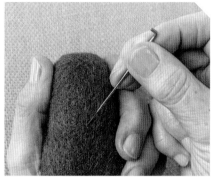

2 Cover with approximately 6g (⅕oz) of brown wool and needle, using a 40 twisted needle, adding more fibres to build up the body.

3 Buttocks Needle felt two small soft round pads using the 40 triangle needle. Attach the pads one at a time and needle until each one is firm and rounded.

4 Arms Make a hole through the top of the body with a bradawl. Spread the middle of the 16cm (6¼in) wire with glue and thread it through the hole. Use the 38 triangle needle to work into the wool around the wire entry and exit to firm it up.

5 Needle one end of a thin length of wool into the upper body to anchor it, then glue the wire. Wrap the wool down the wire, finishing 1cm (½in) from the end.

6 Wrap the arm up and down with lengths of wool, building it up gradually and then add a little more wool around the shoulder area. Use the 38 triangle needle to firm up the wool. Repeat for the other arm.

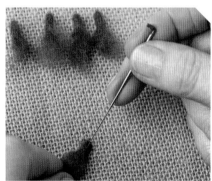

7 Hands Use a 40 triangle needle to needle felt five small sausages for the fingers and thumb. Take care when working this small.

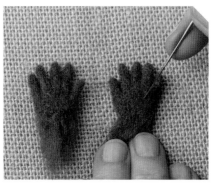

8 Lay the fingers on the pad with the thumb placed slightly lower. Lay some wool over the base of the fingers and needle felt until firm for the palm.

9 Flip, add some more wool and sculpt the hand shape until it is firm and matches the template. Make two hands.

10 Make a hole in the hand, glue the arm wire and push the wire into the hole. Needle around the wrists with the 38 triangle needle, adding more wool if necessary to make sure the join is firm.

11 Legs Roll 7g (¼oz) of wool into a sausage and needle felt the end with the 40 triangle needle for the foot until it is round. Needle felt the bottom flat. Continue needle felting the foot in this way until the flat side measures 4cm (1½in).

12 Bend the wool and needle into the bend to create the heel. Make sure that the bottom is at right angles to the remaining sausage leg so your doll will stand.

13 Continue needle felting up the leg, sculpting it to match the template, until it is firm. Repeat for the other leg.

14 Boots and socks Needle felt a layer of lavender wool onto the feet, using a 40 triangle needle.

15 Lay a 9cm (3½in) length of white wool on your pad for a sock top. Needle felt the strip with the five-needle tool, flipping every now and then to firm it up.

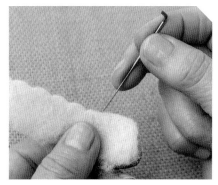

16 Neaten the top edge (see page 42) with the 40 triangle needle before repeatedly needling into it every 5mm (¼in) to create the scalloped edge.

17 Steam iron the strip to neaten, leaving the loose ends, before wrapping it around the ankle. Needle the loose ends into the leg to secure. Needle the joins together at the back.

18 Repeat steps 1 and 2 on page 42 using lavender wool and follow the template for size to create the boot collar.

19 Wrap around the ankle and needle to create a smooth join. Repeat for the other sock and boot.

20 Boot bows To make a white bow for each foot follow step 5 on page 110 for the hair bows. Glue them into place.

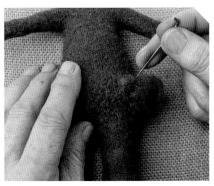

21 Attaching the legs Splay out the loose fibres and press one leg onto the body. Needle the fibres firmly in, adding more wool and filling in any soft areas to create a firm leg. Repeat with the other leg.

Tip

You may have to add a little wool to the bottom of the boots to even up the soles so that your doll will stand.

Woolly wardrobe

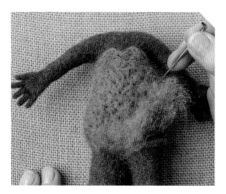

1 Dress Outline and then fill in the costume with lavender wool. Attach the wool with the 40 triangle needle before smoothing the surface with the twisted needle.

2 Wet-felted skirt Prepare your working area as described on page 28. On top of the bubble wrap lay radiating wisps of lavender Merino wool in a 14cm (5½in) circle, overlapping the fibres for a good coverage.

3 Add a smaller even circle of lavender coarse wool on top. Now follow steps 2–11 on pages 43 and 44.

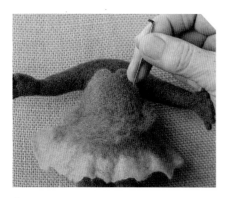

4 While the skirt is wet, slip your doll into it. Let it dry then needle a little lavender coarse wool around the top of the skirt to cover the join.

5 Collar Lay a small amount of white wool on the pad and use the tip of your 40 triangle needle to gently arrange it into the collar shape.

6 Needle felt it flat with the 40 triangle needle and then the five-needle tool, flipping it and rubbing it to speed up the felting. Needle the outer edges between your fingers to neaten.

7 Needle into the collar at 5mm (¼in) intervals to create the scalloped edge then steam iron it.

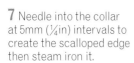

Attaching the head and collar

1 Use a bradawl to make a 3cm (1⅛in) hole in the head and the body. Glue the ends of a 7cm (2¾in) length of wire and push one end into the head and the other into the body, leaving a 1cm (½in) gap for the neck.

2 Once the glue has set hard, wrap the visible neck wire loosely with wool and use a 38 triangle needle to needle the fibres into the body and the head to secure.

3 Wrap the collar around the shoulders and glue to secure. Glue a button over the join.

Rabbit

1 Needle felt a 2g (¹⁄₁₆oz) ball of wool for the head. Needle felt a smaller soft ball for the nose and attach it to the head. Needle repeatedly on either side of the nose to create the eye sockets.

2 Needle felt the body shape using 2g (¹⁄₁₆oz) of wool, leaving loose fibres at the top.

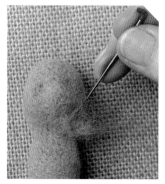

3 Press the head onto the body and needle the loose fibres until the join is secure and smooth.

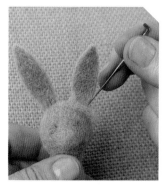

4 Needle felt the rabbit ears, splay out the fibres and attach them to the head.

5 Needle felt four small sausages for the arms and legs and attach them.

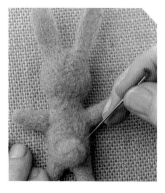

6 Needle felt a small ball for the tail and attach it.

7 Make holes for the eyes, insert the glued eye wires and then needle felt a small triangle for the nose with pink Merino wool.

8 Use black Merino wool wisps to add the mouth details.

9 Gently brush pink pastel powder around the eyes, the nose and the inner ears and, for that finishing touch, glue a ribbon bow to the neck.

As Kawaii means adorable and loveable in popular Japanese culture, we have loved choosing pretty colours for Kate's friend: Cute Caroline. She will delight everyone with her big blue eyes, pink dress, and pretty boots. You could create your own look with different coloured wools, so experiment and have some fun.

SILVER SURFER

. . . .

partial armature * capturing an older look * action pose

Age is great fun to capture in needle felting. It is so easy to create wrinkles, thin hair down and make body bits saggy. Be careful though, because sometimes a face can take on a troll-like appearance if you overdo the needle felting. Features can be sculpted and refined when the felting is at a certain stage, just before it is completely firm. You can use this moment to add wrinkles and laughter lines. This active silver surfer is 75 years old and enjoying his favourite pastime. His pose contains a charge of dynamic energy with his shirt and hair flowing in the wind as he surfs the wavy sea. Sid's top clothes are wet felted using a resist method so there are no seams and no sewing.

Finished size

- 28cm (11in) tall

What you need

SID
- Templates for size and shape (see pages 168–169)
- Foam pad
- Digital scales
- Core wool: 20g (¾oz)
- Yarn
- Coarse wool: approximately 50g (1¾oz) flesh-coloured, 2.5g (1/12oz) white, small amounts of light grey and black
- Felting needles: 40 triangle, 38 triangle, 40 twisted
- Three-needle tool
- Five-needle tool
- Curved embroidery scissors
- Bradawl
- Two 5mm (¼in) wired-backed glass eyes: brown
- Strong clear glue
- Soft pastel: red

- Craft knife
- Small paintbrush
- Acid-free fixative
- Knitting needle
- Wire: **arms** 22cm (8⅝in) length of 1.25mm (18 gauge), **legs and neck** 34cm (13½in) and 7cm (2¾in) lengths of 1.6mm (16 gauge)
- Wire cutters
- Round-nosed pliers

WET-FELTED SHIRT AND SHORTS
- Templates (see page 170)
- Merino wool: **shirt** 6g (1/5oz) pale blue, **shorts** 5g (1/6oz) dark blue
- Old towel
- For the shirt resist, a piece of foam underlay, flexible thick acetate or thin plastic
- Bubble wrap
- Ballpoint pen
- Netting

- Olive soap
- Grater
- Felting bulb spray, water sprinkler, or old plastic bottle with holes
- Wet felting tool
- Scissors
- Rolling pin or a length of pipe insulation
- Bowl

SURFBOARD
- Template (see page 168)
- Thick card 27 x 20cm (10¾ x 8in)
- Craft knife
- Strong clear glue
- Sandpaper
- Acrylic paint: red, blue
- Paintbrush
- Balsa wood: two small rectangles 5mm (¼in) thick
- Wooden base
- Glue gun

Head

1 Referring to the template, tightly roll 7g (¼oz) of core wool and wrap it with yarn to create an inner core for the head (see page 50).

2 Cover the core loosely with wool and needle it evenly all over. Use the 40 triangle needle and then the five-needle tool to speed up the felting and finally the twisted needle to smooth.

3 Needle felt a 5g (⅙oz) soft pad and press it on to the back of the head. Needle felt it to a smooth finish to create the skull shape.

Tip

When sculpting a face, do not needle the features too firmly to start with. Keep them soft and pliable until they are all in place. Then you can further sculpt into them to form the final features.

Features

1 Referring to the templates (see page 169) needle felt the nose, nostrils, brows, cheeks and jowls, upper lip, chin and lower lip and lower eyelids. Attach them in the order described in the following steps.

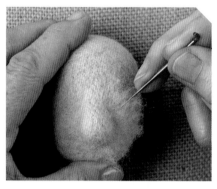

2 Nose Splay out the loose fibres, press the nose onto the face and carefully needle the fibres in to achieve a smooth join.

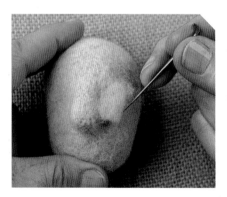

3 Attach one nostril end to the base of the nose.

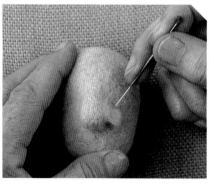

4 Bend it round and needle the other end to the side of the nose. Needle the nostril to shape it and firm it up. Repeat for the second nostril.

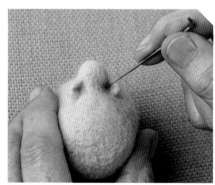

5 Needle up the nostrils to shrink them and further shape the nose.

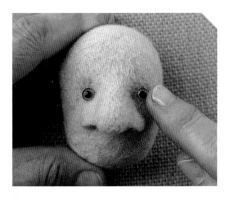
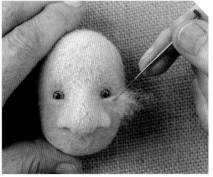

6 Eyes Using the 40 triangle needle, repeatedly needle the two eye sockets, make the holes for the eye wires with a bradawl, then glue and insert the eyes.

7 Attach an eyelid beneath each eye, needling the strip so that it partly covers the iris.

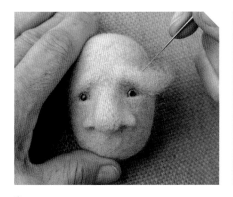
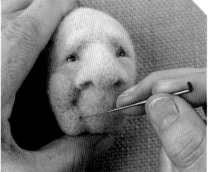
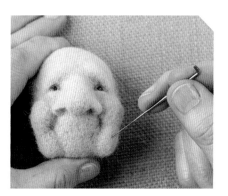

8 Lay one soft fluffy brow over the eye at an angle and, using a 40 triangle needle, needle it into the face with a smooth join. Repeat for the other brow.

9 Cheeks Press cheeks and jowls onto the face then continue to needle felt the cheeks until they are firm and round with a smooth join.

10 Work down the sides of the face, sculpting and firming the jowls.

11 Mouth Attach the top lip just under the nose.

12 Attach the lower lip and chin, leaving a gap between the lips.

13 Fill in the gap between the lips with a little black wool.

14 Add two small balls of white for the two front teeth.

15 Ears Needle felt two ear shapes on your pad. Attach the ears then needle into the centre of each one to make them lay flat against the head.

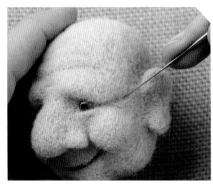

16 Needle lines across his forehead using the 38 triangle needle to create a few wrinkles. Needle a few laughter lines at the sides of the eyes.

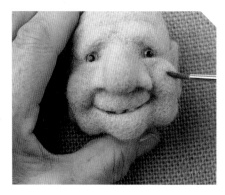

17 Finishing touches Add a gentle blush of pastel powder to the cheeks, chin, nose and inner ears (see page 55).

18 Add the eyebrows, beard and hair with grey wool, leaving it fluffy and flyaway. Put the head aside.

Body

1 Using 13g (⁷⁄₁₆oz) of core wool create a knotted inner core to match the template (see page 51).

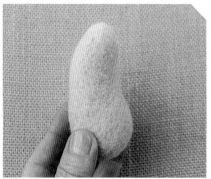

2 Cover the body with approximately 8g (¼oz) of wool. Using the three-needle tool and the 40 triangle needle build up the shoulders and the tummy until they match the template.

3 Arms Make a hole through the top of the body with a bradawl (with the help of a knitting needle if the hole is too small). Push a 22cm (8⅝in) length of wire through the hole, pull it back, glue the middle section and push it back through again. Needle round the entry and exit points to tighten the fibres.

4 Starting from the shoulder, glue the wire and wrap the arm up and down with lengths of wool, building it up gradually. Leave 1cm (½in) of base wire at the end. Add a little more wool around the shoulder area iif necessary.

5 Using the 38 triangle needle, needle the wrapped arm to neaten and shape. Then gently pinprick with the twisted needle to smooth.

6 Hands For each hand, use the 40 triangle needle to needle felt four small sausages for the fingers and one smaller sausage for the thumb.

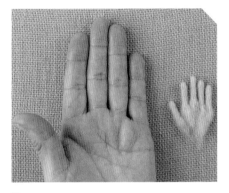

7 Arrange the fingers and thumbs on the pad, using your own hand as reference for positioning.

8 Needle more wool to the base of the fingers to hold them together and create the palm.

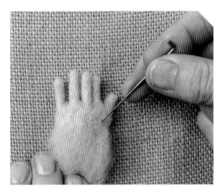

9 Turn the hand over, add more fibres and needle felt until smooth and you have achieved the correct shape, adding more wool where necessary.

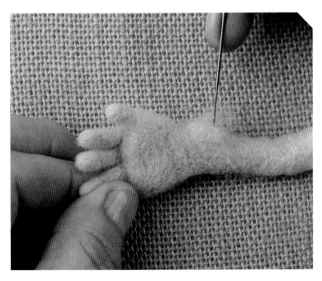

10 Make a hole in the hand, glue the arm wire and push it into the hole. Use the 38 triangle needle to needle the loose fibres firmly into the wrist. Repeat with the other hand.

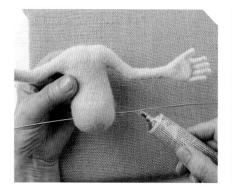

11 Legs Make a hole through the bottom of the body and feed the 34cm (13½in) length of wire through. Enlarge the hole with a knitting needle if necessary. Pull the wire out and glue the centre then thread it back through the hole.

12 Needle round the wire entry and exit to secure. Bend one leg wire down, glue and wrap with lengths of wool down to 3cm (1⅛in) from the end. Build up the thigh with more wool.

Tip

To speed up the process, roll the legs between your hands now and again.

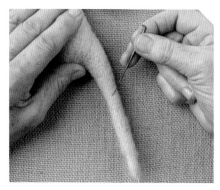

13 When you have finished wrapping, needle down the leg to smooth the surface with the 40 twisted needle. Repeat for the other leg.

14 Feet Use 3g (¹⁄₁₀oz) of wool to needle felt the foot shape (see template on page 169) until it is very firm, using the 40 triangle needle.

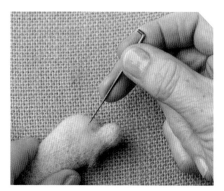

16 Needle felt the toe strip, then mark the individual toes by needling three lines into the strip.

15 Needle felt the big toe. Splay out the fibres, press it onto the foot and needle to secure.

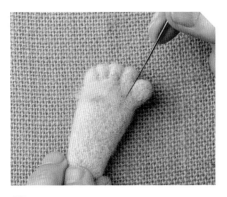

17 Splay out the fibres, push the toes onto the foot and sculpt with your needle to neaten. Repeat to make a second foot.

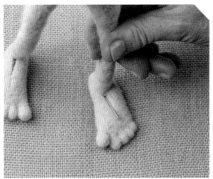

18 Bend the last 3cm (1⅛in) of each leg to make the feet. Using the craft knife carefully, make a slit in the top of each foot, glue the wires and slide them into the slits.

19 Wrap more wool around the ankles and over the slits to secure the wire. Needle in and neaten.

Attaching the head

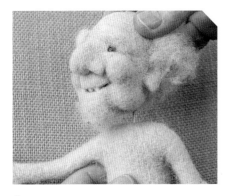

1 Make a hole in the head and neck and insert the 7cm (2¾in) glued wire, leaving a 1cm (½in) gap for the neck.

2 Wrap the neck wire loosely with a little wool and use the 38 triangle needle to push the fibres up into the head and down into the body to firm up and secure.

Woolly wardrobe

1 Vest Use thin lengths of white wool to outline the neck and armholes then fill in down to the waist with more white wool.

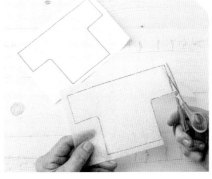

2 Wet-felted shirt Referring to the template (see page 170), trace the shirt pattern onto the underlay and cut out the resist.

3 Prepare your wet felting work station (see page 28). Use small pulls of pale blue Merino wool to cover the resist and felt the shirt, following steps 2–18 on pages 45–47.

4 While still damp, dress your doll. Arrange the shirt to give it a flyaway look, and leave to dry.

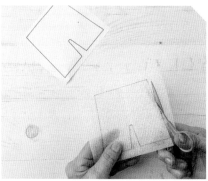

5 Wet-felted shorts Trace the shorts template (see page 170) onto a piece of underlay and cut out a resist using the same technique as for the shirt.

6 Cover the resist with layers of dark blue wool. Felt as for the shirt.

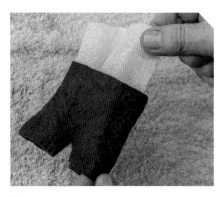

7 Once felted, cut across the top of the shorts and the bottoms of the legs and remove the resist.

8 Complete the shorts following the shirt instructions on pages 45–47, slide the damp shorts onto your doll and leave to dry.

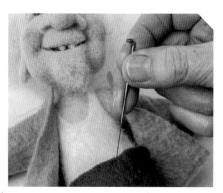

9 Needle the top of the shorts into the doll's body to shrink the waistband so that it fits.

Surfboard

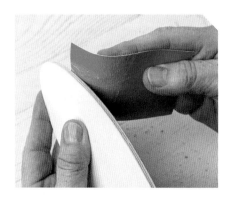
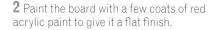

1 Referring to the template, cut out three surfboard shapes from thick card and glue them together. When dry, sand the edges until they are smooth and rounded.

2 Paint the board with a few coats of red acrylic paint to give it a flat finish.

3 Using the craft knife, cut two small rectangles of 5mm (¼in) thick balsa wood or card. Glue them together and sand across the top front edge.

4 Glue the rectangle to the base, then paint with blue acrylic paint.

5 Use a glue gun to glue the surfboard to the base.

6 Pose Sid, then glue the bottoms of his feet and press them onto the surfboard.

Meet Sid's sister – our golden oldie Glorious Gloria who is having fun practising for the Felty Towers annual Woolympics. We followed the instructions for Sid, making Gloria more shapely with make-up, flyaway hair and pretty accessories. For her handbag see the templates on page 170 and follow the step-by-step bag instructions on pages 73 and 74. For her skateboard, make and assemble as shown using the skateboard template (see page 170) and diagram (see page 168), then paint.

PERFECT PORTRAITS

partial armature * needle felting a lookalike

Over the years our commissions have included requests to needle felt mini versions of loved ones, which initially was a bit of a challenge. After exploring different ways of working we have now developed a few tips to help you with the leap from reality to a lookalike woolly personality. First, gather some information about your subject. Be sure to have 'full body and face' photographs – and one of a favourite outfit helps. Find out what they do for a living, whether they have a pet, and ask about their hobbies and interests, too. If you are doing a commission, discuss the reasons for the request. It could be for a special event like a birthday. For a bit of fun we have needle felted ourselves – without any wrinkles or crinkles of course! Follow the instructions here, then have a go at making a selfie. Your own doll will be different, so do adjust the templates to suit the model.

Finished size

- 30cm (11¾in)

What you need

DOLL

- Photograph of face
- Tracing paper
- Pencil
- Templates for size and shape (see page 171)
- Foam pad
- Digital scales
- Coarse wool: approximately 45g (1½oz) flesh-coloured, 4g (⅐oz) dark blue and light blue carded together, 6g (⅕oz) turquoise, 6g (⅕oz) black, small amounts of dark turquoise, white and blue
- Core wool: 6g (⅕oz)
- Merino wool: **hair** 3g (1/10oz) carded dark, light and mid brown
- Felting needles: 40 triangle, 38 triangle, 40 twisted
- Three-needle tool
- Five-needle tool
- Bradawl
- Carders
- Two 3mm (⅛in) wire-backed glass eyes: blue
- Strong clear glue
- Soft pastel: red
- Craft knife
- Small paintbrush
- Acid-free fixative
- Wire: **arms** 25cm (9¾in) length of 1.25mm (18 gauge), **legs** 36cm (14¼in) length of 1.25mm (18 gauge), **neck** 6cm (2½in) length of 1.6mm (16 gauge)
- Wire cutters
- Knitting needle
- Embroidery thread: blue
- Tapestry needle
- Curved embroidery scissors
- Steam iron
- Hair spray

SHEEP

- Templates (see page 172)
- Coarse wool: approximately 7g (¼oz) cream
- Merino wool: small amount of black
- Wensleydale wool: 3g (1/10oz)
- Two 2mm (1/16in) wire-backed glass eyes: black
- Soft pastel: pale pink

Capturing a likeness

Observation is key when capturing a likeness, so really study the features before you start needle felting them. The features are very small, so be careful of your fingers as you are needling.

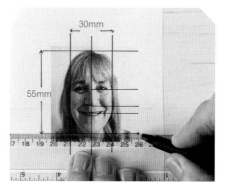

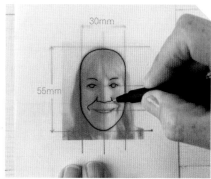

1 Print a photograph of the face to measure approximately 5.5cm (2¼in) from the top of the head to the chin and mark the measurements of the features to help you with sizing.

2 Trace the head shape and features. This will be the size to work to.

Head

1 Needle felt the head using 4g (⅐oz) of wool and the three-needle tool, then the 40 triangle needle to neaten. Needle one side of the head flat for the face. Match to the template.

2 To create the more realistic skull shape needle felt a soft 3g (⅒oz) pad and attach it to the upper back of the head. Use the twisted needle to smooth the join.

Features

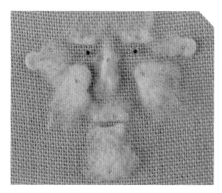

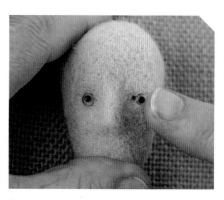

1 Referring to the template, needle felt the nose, cheeks, chin, upper and lower lips, eyelids and ears.

2 Nose Splay out the fibres around the nose, press it onto the face and use a 40 triangle needle to needle a smooth join.

3 Eyes Make two eye holes with a bradawl, glue the eye wires and press one eye firmly into each hole.

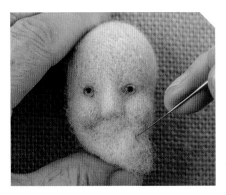

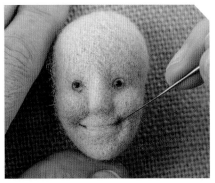

4 Cheeks and chin Press each cheek onto the face one at a time and needle them into the face. Attach the chin and needle the loose fibres with the twisted needle making sure the joins are smooth.

5 Mouth Attach the upper and lower lips and needle some white wool between the lips for the teeth. Needle a wisp of black in the corners of the mouth to create shadows.

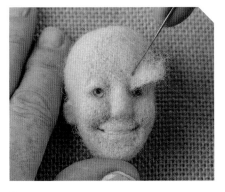

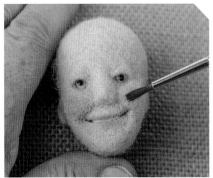

6 Needle in the ears and upper eyelids. Working with these small features takes time, but it is worth it!

7 Brush over the cheeks, eyelids, chin and lips lightly with a little red pastel powder.

Body

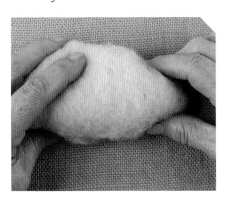

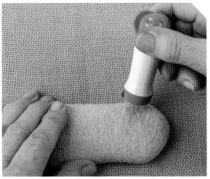

1 Lay 11g (⅜oz) of wool on the pad and firmly roll it into a sausage slightly larger than the template.

2 Use the three-needle tool then 40 triangle needle and the five-needle tool to shape the body, rubbing the wool firmly between your hands every now and then to speed up the felting.

3 Breasts Needle felt two soft balls for the chest and following steps 10 and 11 on page 38, attach them to the chest.

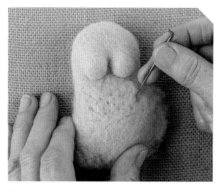

4 Needle felt a 2.5g (1/12oz) soft tummy pad, attach it to the body and needle until smooth, matching the shape of your model and adding more wool if necessary.

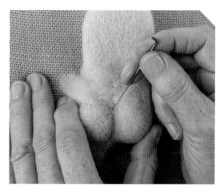

5 Needle felt two 2.5g (1/12oz) buttocks and attach them one at a time.

6 Arms Make a hole through the top of the body with a bradawl. Spread glue along the middle of the 25cm (9¾in) length of wire and thread it through the hole. Needle around the wire ends with a 38 triangle needle to tighten the wool.

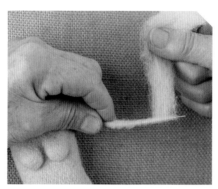

7 Glue the wires and wrap them with lengths of wool, building them up gradually.

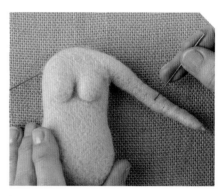

8 Continue to glue and wrap the wire in this way, shaping the arm so that it is thicker towards the top. Needle felt the arm to smooth. Repeat for the other arm.

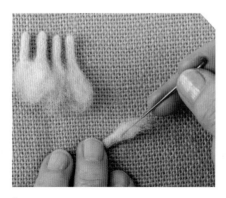

9 Hands Needle felt four small sausage fingers and a smaller sausage thumb with the 40 triangle needle.

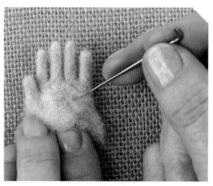

10 Lay four fingers and a thumb on the pad. To create the palm needle a small pad of wool over their loose ends.

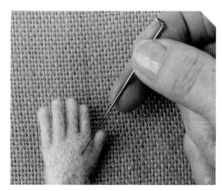

11 Turn the hand over and add more wool, needling it until it is firm. Build up the hand adding more wool where necessary, sculpting it to the right shape.

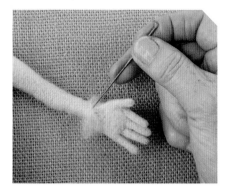

12 Make a hole in the hand with a bradawl, glue the arm wire and press it into the hole. Needle the loose fibres from the hand into the wrist to secure. Needle the join to firm and smooth. Add a little extra wool if necessary. Repeat for the other arm.

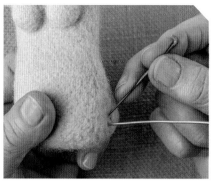

13 Legs Glue the centre of the 36cm (14¼in) length of wire, thread it through the lower half of the body and needle around the wires with a 38 triangle needle to secure it.

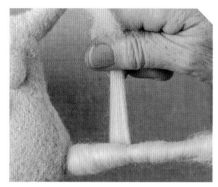

14 Following the technique opposite as described for the arms, wrap the wires this time with lengths of core wool.

15 Bend the wires down and bend the last 3.5cm (1¼in) of each wire to create the feet. If your model has a slightly larger frame, add more wool wraps to the thighs.

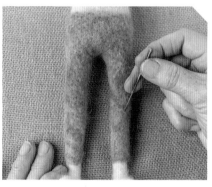

16 Cover the bottom and legs with carded blue wool. Work down to the ankles.

17 Needle some turquoise wool round each ankle for the socks and then cover each foot with black wool, building it up to create the foot shape. Needle the bottom flat so that your doll will stand without falling over.

18 Needle felt the boot tongue and attach it to the front of the boot top.

19 Using a small amount of wool needle felt the boot collar, wrap it around the ankle and needle the join so that it is smooth. Complete the second boot.

Tip

If you needle felt deeply, sometimes strands of white core wool will show through the black felt. You can colour these with a black felt tip pen.

20 Sew the laces onto the boots (see diagram on page 92).

Attaching the head

 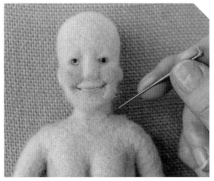

1 Use a bradawl to make a deep hole into the top of the body and another up into the head. Glue both ends of a 6cm (2½in) length of wire. Push one end into the body and one into the head leaving a gap for the neck. Needle around each hole to secure the wire.

2 Once the glue has set hard, wrap the visible neck wire loosely with wool. Needle the fibres into the body and head to secure.

T-shirt

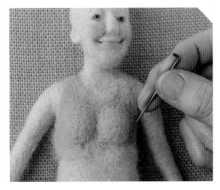 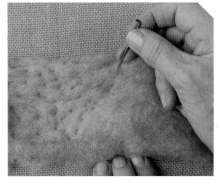 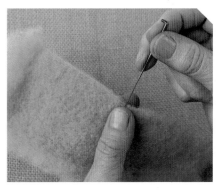

1 Using the 40 triangle needle, edge the neck with turquoise wool then work down the body to just below the breast, filling the area with more wool.

2 Shape a 3.5g (⅛oz) rectangle of turquoise wool on your pad so that it measures 18 x 6cm (7⅛ x 2½in). Needle felt with the 40 triangle needle, flipping it frequently until it firms, leaving the lower and side edges as loose fibres. Continue with the five-needle tool and then the twisted needle to neaten.

3 Needle into the top edge to neaten and tuck in any loose fibres. The wool can be sandwiched between a piece of folded card to protect your fingers (see Tip on page 42).

4 Referring to the template needle felt two semi-circular sleeves in the same way.

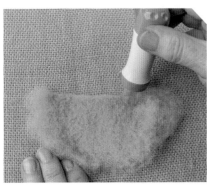 

5 Needle felt small blue, dark turquoise and white circles over the t-shirt pieces, then trim across each circle to make them flat.

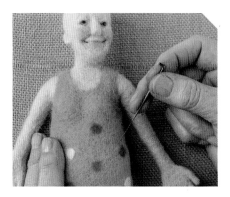

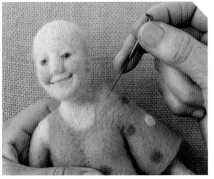

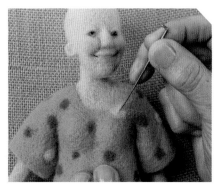

6 Steam iron the three pieces (not the loose ends) then attach the t-shirt strip just under the bust. Needle felt until the join is smooth and the bodice runs into the t-shirt strip. Needle felt the join at the back of the doll.

7 Wrap each sleeve around the upper arms. Needle the loose fibres into the arms and shoulders.

8 Needle felt more wool spots over the top of the t-shirt to complete the design and then work over the whole surface with a twisted needle to smooth.

Hair

The instructions below are for Judy's hairstyle. It is easy to adapt hair using this technique by trimming locks once the wool lengths have been secured. If your model has curly hair you could use Wensleydale wool. If you are not sure what you would like, browse through the projects and choose a hairstyle.

1 Pull out some smooth 14cm (5½in) lengths of carded Merino wool and fold them to create layered pieces.

2 Starting at the back, place the fold across the base of the head and needle felt it to secure with the 40 triangle needle. Complete a row from ear to ear.

3 Needle layers in rows approximately 1cm (½in) apart. Work the first row to the top of the head (the fringe line).

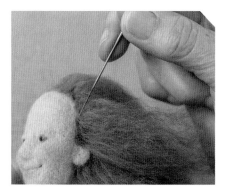

4 Needle felt more layers on each side of the head.

5 Needle a final fringe layer at the front.

6 Use your needle tip to smooth the hair. Lightly needle it to shape and flatten, then start the haircut!

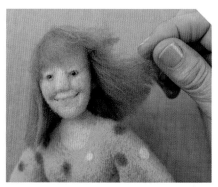

7 Arrange the hair to give some movement, then lightly spray with hair spray.

Sheep

Follow the instructions for making the rabbit body and features on page 116.

1 Referring to the templates, use 7g (¼oz) of wool to needle felt the head, the body, the ears and the four legs.

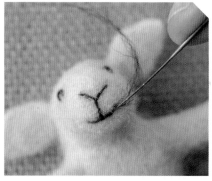

2 Join all the body parts together, attach the eyes and then needle felt the nose and mouth details.

3 Colour the nose and inner ears with pale pink pastel powder, then needle Wensleydale curls over your sheep.

Needle felting our woolly selves has been an entertaining challenge – what fun we have had with this enjoyable project. Reflecting a love of books and art, our Roz doll has loved having her portrait painted by Vincent van Gogh. Whether you choose to needle felt selfies, loved ones, friends or famous people, the techniques are the same. Just change the colours and accessories to make the dolls your own.

MOTHER EARTH

full armature * needle felting on polystyrene * adding a display base

Protector of our planet, healer and bringer of new life, Janet Planet cares for us all while preserving nature and safeguarding our precious world. With her green fingers and flowing robe she is needle felted onto a full wire armature. This means she can be posed easily and is strong enough to carry the whole world in her hands. Janet's leg wires are secured in a wooden base to help her stand, her face is sculpted to add character, and her skirt and headdress are wet felted to create a delicately draped organic look. Wool is needled into a polystyrene ball to create the planet Earth.

Finished size

• 34cm (13½in) without the base

What you need

MOTHER EARTH
• Templates for size and shape (see page 173)
• Wire armature: two 45cm (17¾in) lengths and one 11cm (4⅜in) length of 1.6mm (16 gauge), to secure – 30cm (11¾in) and 70cm (27⅝in) lengths of 0.4mm (27 gauge)
• Wire cutters
• Round-nosed pliers
• Masking tape
• Strong clear glue
• Digital scales
• Core wool: 10g (⅓oz)
• Coarse wool: approximately 50g (1¾oz) flesh-coloured, 14g (½oz) green, 2g (⅟₁₆oz) grey
• Merino wool: 5g (⅟₆oz) green for the bodice
• Foam pad

• Felting needles: 40 triangle, 38 triangle, 36 triangle, 40 twisted
• Three-needle tool
• Five-needle tool
• Curved embroidery scissors
• Bradawl
• Two 5mm (¼in) wire-backed glass eyes: brown
• Soft pastels: red, green
• Craft knife
• Small paintbrush
• Acid-free fixative
• Steam iron
• Base: two wooden discs 1.5cm (¾in) thick
• Drill with 1.6mm bit
• Dyed scrim: a small length
• Strong cotton
• Charms: bronzed metal tree of life, two miniature glass bottles
• Miniature paper flowers

WET-FELTED SKIRT AND HEADDRESS
• Old towel
• Bubble wrap
• Merino wool: approximately 10g (⅓oz) green, 5g (⅟₆oz) dark turquoise and small pulls of cerise
• Wool nepps: blue, salmon
• Silk: salmon
• Netting
• Olive soap
• Grater
• Felting bulb spray, water sprinkler, or old plastic bottle with holes
• Wet felting tool
• Rolling pin or a length of pipe insulation
• Dressmaking scissors
• Piece of foam approximately 14 x 6 x 2cm (5½ x 2½ x ¾in)
• Bowl

Armature

When working with a full armature we always work with a stronger, thicker 36 triangle needle to avoid breakages.

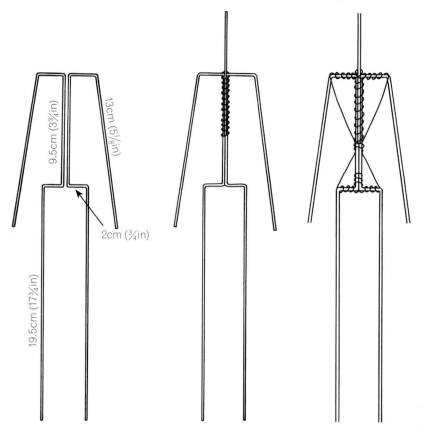

Diagram 1

Use the round-nosed pliers to help bend the wire to the above measurements.

Diagram 2

Wrap thin wire around the thicker frame to secure.

Diagram 3

Wrap and strengthen the shoulders and lower body with the thin wire.

Diagram 4

Add more wool to the figure if needed, rounding contours and finishing off with the smoothing technique (see page 31).

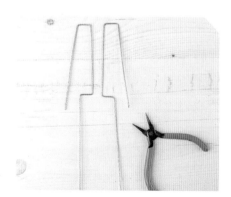

1 Bend the two 45cm (17¾in) lengths of wire to the shape of the armature (see diagram 1).

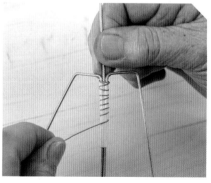

2 Add the 11cm (4⅜in) head wire so that 5cm (2in) extends at the top. Wrap the wires with masking tape to secure and then wrap them again with thin wire to strengthen.

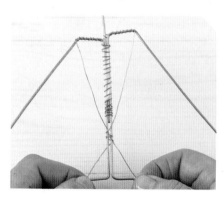

3 Wrap the middle of a 70cm (27⅝in) length of thin wire once around the neck wire. Referring to diagram 3, wrap each wire end along the shoulder, bring both wires down to the waist, cross them and then out to the hips, wrapping them along the hip wires before a final wrap up the centre wires.

4 Twist the wire ends securely together and trim any excess ends.

5 Body Smear the wires with glue as you work, then gradually wrap the armature with lengths of core wool. When you come to the end of a length of core wool, needle the end into the wrapped section to secure.

6 Build up the armature with wraps of wool in this way until it resembles a basic body shape, needling with the 36 triangle needle as you wrap to secure the fibres.

Tip

Every now and again needle felt the core wool with the 36 triangle needle so that it tightens round the wire and becomes firm.

7 Using a 38 triangle needle, start adding flesh-coloured wool.

8 Using approximately 14g (½oz) of wool, gradually build up the shoulders and buttocks to refine the shape.

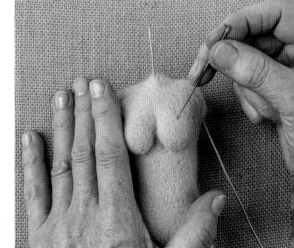

9 Needle felt two breasts separately using the 40 triangle needle, and attach them to the chest using the 38 triangle needle.

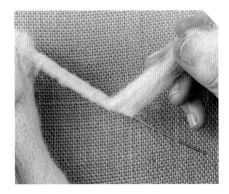

10 Needle a length of wool into the shoulder. Then, working on one arm at a time, smear the wire with glue and wrap down to 2cm (¾in) from the end.

11 Build up the arm with more wool wraps and then needle a small soft pad for the elbow and attach it using the 38 triangle needle.

12 Work in the same way for the legs, wrapping the wires and building them up to the required shape, finishing 3cm (1⅛in) from the end.

Head

1 Tightly roll an 8g (¼oz) ball of wool and needle felt it to match the template using the three-needle tool, then the 40 triangle needle and the 40 twisted needle to neaten.

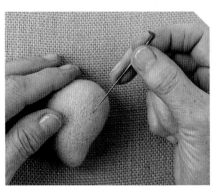

2 Needle felt a 4.5g (⅙oz) soft pad and attach it to the upper back of the head to create the skull shape. Smooth with the twisted needle.

Features

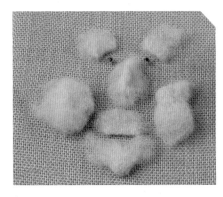

1 Referring to the templates, needle felt all the features with the 40 triangle needle: the nose, cheeks and jowls, top lip, chin and brows.

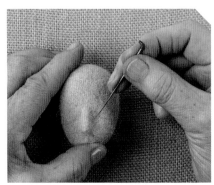

2 Nose Splay out the loose fibres, press the nose onto the face and needle to create a smooth join.

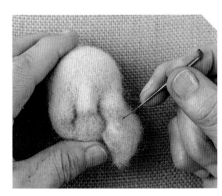

3 Cheeks and jowls Attach these in the same way, needling into the cheeks to make them rounded and firm.

4 Mouth and chin Place the top lip under the nose and use the needle to sculpt the shape into a smile.

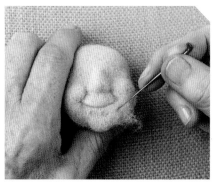

5 Attach the chin to the bottom of the face and needle to create a smooth join between the chin and jowls.

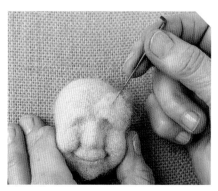

6 Eyes Attach one brow above each eye, slanting them down to create a serene look.

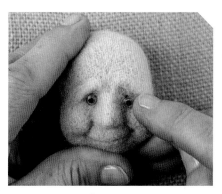

7 Make holes with a bradawl, glue the eye wires and insert the eyes.

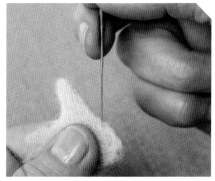

8 Pointy ears Using a small amount of wool for each ear, needle felt the two ear shapes on the pad. Needle around the edges to neaten.

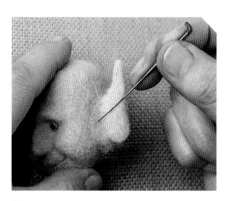

9 Splay out the fibres, press them onto the head and needle the loose fibres until secure.

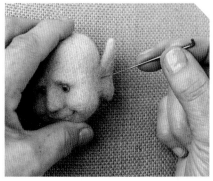

10 Needle into each ear to position them flat against the head.

11 Colouring the face Use a paintbrush to add a gentle blush of red pastel powder to the cheeks, chin, lips, inner ears and round the eyes, then dust the tips of the ears with green pastel powder.

12 Hands Needle felt four fingers and a smaller thumb using the 40 triangle needle.

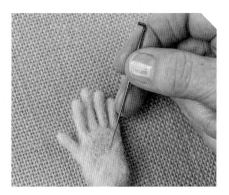

13 Place a small bundle of fibres at the base of four fingers and a thumb, then needle until firm to create the palm (use your own hand as reference).

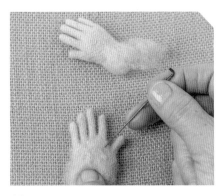

14 Turn the hand over and repeat this on the back, sculpting the wool to match the template. Make a second hand.

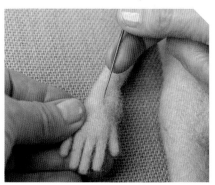

15 Make a hole in the hand, glue the arm wire and push it into the hole. Needle the loose hand fibres into the wrist and needle to secure and firm up. Repeat for the other hand and then use the twisted needle to smooth the join.

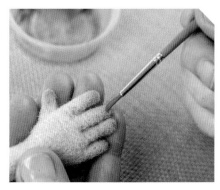

16 Dust the ends of the fingers and thumbs with green pastel powder.

Boots

1 Using 2.5g (1/12oz) of green wool and the 40 triangle needle, needle felt the basic boot shape. Use the template for reference.

2 Needle a thin layer of turquoise wool onto the bottom for the sole. Make two.

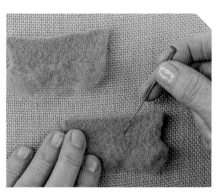

3 Needle felt two 2g (1/16oz) boot collars, then steam iron. (See making a flat strip on page 42.)

4 Make a hole in each boot with the bradawl, glue the leg wires and slide the boots up the wires.

5 Wrap a collar round each boot and needle to smooth and secure with a 38 triangle needle.

Woolly wardrobe

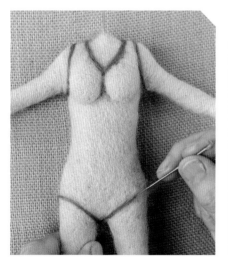

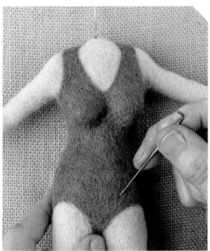

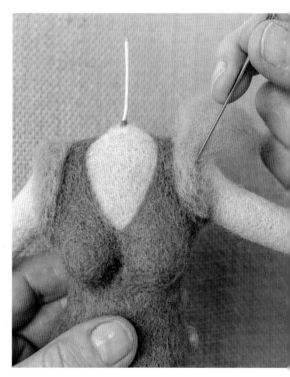

1 Bodice Outline the neck, arms and legs of the body with thin lengths of green Merino wool to mark the edges of the bodice.

2 Fill in with more wool and needle until smooth with the twisted needle.

3 Lightly needle some coarse green fibres around the two arm holes.

Attaching the head

1 Make a hole in the head with the bradawl, spread the head wire with glue, then press the head onto the wire so that 1cm (½in) of wire remains visible.

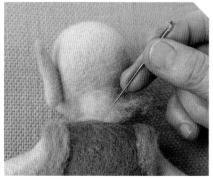

2 Wrap the visible neck wire loosely with wool, then carefully needle felt the wool into the body and up into the head to secure, using a 38 triangle needle.

3 Needle to secure three thin lengths of grey wool to the pad. Braid the lengths leaving loose fibres at the top and bottom.

Hair

1 Needle felt the braid to the side of the head and add more grey wool to complete the hairstyle.

2 Use grey wool to add fluffy eyebrows above the eyes.

Wet-felted skirt and headband

It is time to do some wet felting, so first set up your working base (see page 28).

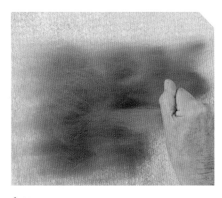

1 Skirt Overlap horizontal wispy pulls of green Merino wool on top of the bubble wrap to cover a 20 x 25cm (8 x 9¾in) area.

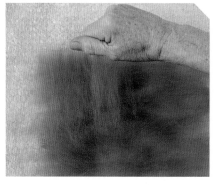

2 Repeat, laying a second layer of wool over the first layer but this time lay it vertically. Work over the top two thirds of the rectangle.

3 Complete the lower third in the same way with dark turquoise and wisps of cerise Merino wool.

4 Sprinkle the lower half of the fibres with wool nepps and then lay down thin wisps of salmon-coloured silk strands adding a few green fibres over them to secure them during the felting process.

5 Lay the netting on top and sprinkle with warm water containing grated soap.

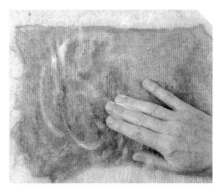

6 Press down on the netting with your hands to make sure the fibres are completely wet. Rub the netting gently in circles for approximately 10 minutes until the fibres bind together.

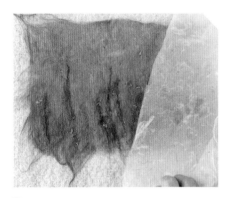

7 Remove the netting and carefully flip the felt over. Replace the netting, repeat steps 6 and 7 once more, then follow steps 7 and 8 on page 44.

8 Wash the piece of felt in warm water and wring out. Wash it in cold water, wring out, spread out and dry.

9 When dry cut the width to 20cm (8in) and cut across the top so that the length measures 17cm (6¾in). Lay it face down and wrap it around a slightly smaller piece of foam, keeping the leftover felted strips for later use.

10 Smear one edge with glue and press the other edge on top and then lightly needle along the glued join.

11 Peel the felt fabric tube away from the foam and slip it onto your doll.

12 Needle felt the top of the skirt into her body just under the bust.

13 Wrap a length of cerise wool around her waist to cover the join and needle it at the back to secure.

14 Wrap her head with one of the left over wet-felted strips and glue the ends together at the back to make a headband. Add more grey wool for the hair if needed.

Storytelling accessories

Janet Planet carries our precious home, the planet Earth, surrounded by cooing doves and woolly fruit. These accessories tell her story. You may want to add more, or create a different character like our woolly witch on page 153. She has been needle felted following the instructions in this project and we have dipped into the Weird and Wonderful project on page 160 to make her ancient spell book.

What you need

PLANET EARTH
• Template for map (see page 172)
• Polystyrene ball: 6cm (2½in) diameter
• Felt tip pen: blue
• Felting needles: 40 triangle, 40 twisted
• Coarse wool: 3g (1/10oz) green, 4g (1/7oz) blue
• Fuzz remover tool

DOVES (FOR EACH BIRD)
• Templates for size and shape (see page 173)
• Felting needles: 40 triangle, 40 twisted
• Coarse wool: approximately 3g (1/10oz) white and 3g (1/10oz) orange
• Merino wool: small pull of black
• Steam iron

FRUIT (FOR EACH PIECE)
• Templates for size and shape (see page 173)
• Felting needles: 40 triangle, 40 twisted
• Coarse wool: small amounts of green and orange
• Merino wool: small amount of black
• Soft pastels: red, orange
• Craft knife
• Small paintbrush
• Acid-free fixative

Planet Earth

Fibres are needled into a polystyrene ball to create the planet. This simple technique can be used to make a whole range of wonderful woolly shapes.

1 Draw the shape of the continents on the ball with a felt tip pen (see diagram on page 172).

(see diagram on page 172)

2 Use the 40 triangle needle to needle green wool into the land areas. Needle shallowly and carefully so as not to over stab the polystyrene.

3 Needle blue wool into all the sea areas around the globe.

4 Roll the ball firmly in your hands to flatten and even out the wool covering.

5 Smooth the surface with angled shallow stabs using the twisted needle. Finally work over your planet with the fuzz remover tool.

Tips

If you needle too aggressively into the polystyrene surface it will disintegrate. Needle evenly and do not repeatedly stab in one area.

Other shapes can be made and attached to a base shape, for example, a cauldron for our woolly witch (see page 153).

(see page 153)

Doves

For the doves you will be creating small shapes, so watch your fingers! When working on this reduced scale the key is to relax and to needle felt slowly, rather than rushing through the instructions.

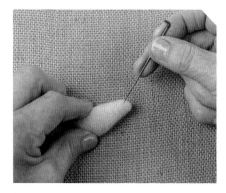

1 Flying dove Referring to the template, tightly roll a small sausage of white wool and needle felt the body with the 40 triangle needle.

2 Needle felt the two wings and tail shapes on the pad (see page 42 for how to felt flat shapes).

3 Needle into the edge of the wings and around the tail every few millimetres to create the scalloped edges (see collar on page 114).

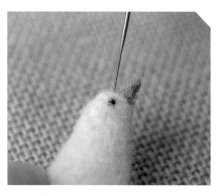

4 Needle two eye dots with thin wisps of black Merino wool, trimming off any excess. Needle felt a small orange cone beak on your pad and attach it to the head.

5 Steam iron the wings and tail avoiding the loose fibres and then splay out the fibres and attach them to the body.

6 Nesting dove Needle felt the body, wings and tail. Attach the wings so that they lie flat to the body and complete the dove following steps 4 and 5 of the flying dove.

If you simply change the colour of a dove and apply the basic principles of body shape and individual characteristics of other birds, you can needle felt different breeds. We have chosen to make a friendly crow who is now our woolly witch's faithful companion.

Fruit

To give a realistic fruity 'blush', blend the mix of pastel colours smoothly into the wool with the paintbrush.

1 Referring to the template, needle felt three green apples, two pears and three oranges using the 40 triangle needle, finishing and smoothing each one with the twisted needle.

2 Add the stalk mark with a small black wisp of Merino wool on each fruit.

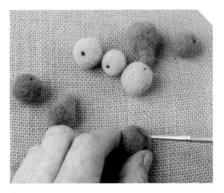

3 Brush over them with red or orange chalk pastel to give a more realistic look. The colours are fixed with acid-free fixative.

Adding a base

1 Glue wooden discs together to create a deep base of approximately 3cm (1⅛in).

2 Pose your doll then hold her over the base. Mark where the two wires touch the base.

3 Drill two vertical holes and insert the glued feet wires.

Finishing touches

1 Wrap a length of scrim around the doll's shoulders.

2 Thread strong cotton through the tree charm and tie it around her neck.

3 Fill the mini bottles with seeds and spices. Thread the bottles onto strong cotton then loop them over the waistband.

4 Glue a small bunch of mini paper flowers to each boot.

5 Arrange and glue the fruit to the base.

6 Glue the planet onto one hand. Glue a flying dove onto the other hand and one to the base. Glue the nesting dove to a shoulder. Pose Mother Earth so that she is looking at the dove.

The instructions for Mother Earth and our woolly witch are the same but we have changed colours and accessories to show how different you can make your doll look. Fiery colours and long dyed Wensleydale locks are perfect for a special magical 'glow'. The cauldron has a polystyrene base and a painted wire handle, and the crow is needle felted with black coarse wool following the dove instructions. To make the book, see page 160.

WEIRD AND WONDERFUL

· ·

let your imagination fly

The magic of wool allows us to fly away with our ideas however quirky they may be, so once you have learnt all the techniques the only limit is your imagination. Remember, there are no rules. In this project Ed Artymus Boodle – Professor of the Absurd, is dressed up for his stage debut in stripy stockings and spectacles with a top hat nesting in his hair. As head of our woolly Felty Towers family, he is delighted to meet you all and is looking forward to helping you with this project. He is also excited about meeting his woolly stage partner Miss Sally Strangelove (see page 161). If you are feeling adventurous add a few of your own ideas and have fun. Happy needle felting.

Finished size

• 24cm (9½in)

What you need

DOLL
• Templates for size and shape (see pages 174–175)
• Digital scales
• Foam pad
• Core wool: 50g (1¾oz)
• Yarn
• Coarse wool: 22g (¾oz) flesh-coloured, 13g (⁷⁄₁₆oz) red, small amounts of black and white
• Merino wool: small amozunts of orange, dark brown, white, 2g (¹⁄₁₆oz) red, 2g (¹⁄₁₆oz) black
• Herdwick wool, approximately 15g (½oz), for hair, eyebrows, moustache and beard
• Felting needles: 40 triangle, 38 triangle, 40 twisted
• Three-needle tool

• Five-needle tool
• Felt tip pen: brown
• Wire: **arms** two 11cm (4⅜in) lengths of 1.25mm (18 gauge), **legs** 44cm (17⅜in) length of 1.6mm (16 gauge)
• Wire cutters
• Round-nosed pliers
• Strong clear glue
• Bradawl
• Craft knife
• Steam iron
• Embroidery thread: black
• Tapestry needle
• Knitting needle
• Curved embroidery scissors
• Heart pin
• Soft pastel: red
• Small paintbrush
• Acid-free fixative

BOOK
• Coarse wool: 4.5g (⅙oz) brown
• Ruler
• Ready-made felt: three 12 x 7cm (4¾ x 2¾in) pieces of cream, 4cm (1½in) square of red
• Sewing needle
• Cotton thread: cream and brown
• Felt tip pen: black

GLASSES
• Template for size and shape (see page 175)
• Wire: 45cm (17¾in) length of 1mm (18 gauge)
• Waxed floral tape
• Acrylic paint: dark red

Head

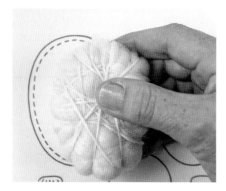

1 Roll 25g (⅞oz) of core wool tightly into an oval, using the dotted lines on the head template for size, and wrap it tightly with yarn to secure.

2 Use the 40 triangle needle to cover the ball with approximately 5g (⅙oz) of flesh-coloured wool. Then use the five-needle tool and the twisted needle to needle it smooth.

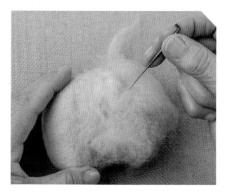

3 Needle felt a 5g (⅙oz) soft pad and press it onto the upper back of the head. Use a 40 triangle needle, then the five-needle tool to create the skull shape.

4 Smooth and finish the surface with the 40 twisted needle.

Features

1 Nose Referring to the templates, use 7g (¼oz) of wool for all the features. For the nose, needle felt a small soft pad using the 40 triangle needle then fold it in half.

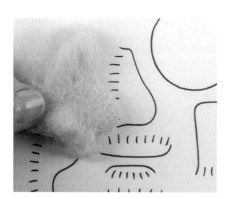

2 Needle repeatedly down the fold (bridge of the nose), fold the bottom up and needle into it to firm up the lower part of the nose until it matches the template.

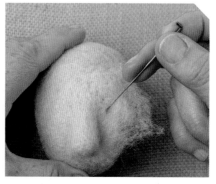

3 Splay out the fibres, press the nose onto the face and needle the loose ends in for a smooth join.

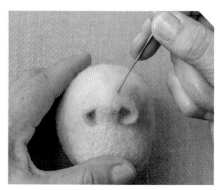

4 Needle felt two nostrils, attach one to either side of the nose, then sculpt and smooth them into the face.

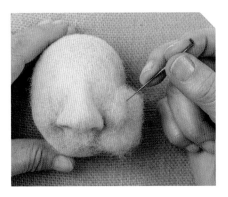

5 Chin and cheeks Softly needle felt the cheeks and attach them to the face.

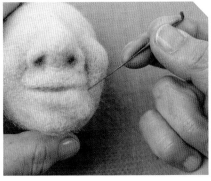

6 Needle felt the chin and attach it. Needle felt the upper and lower lips and attach them leaving a gap between the lips.

7 Fill the gap with white wool and needle until smooth. Add a few black fibres inside the corners of the mouth.

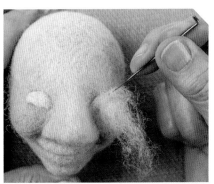

8 Eyes Needle the eye sockets flat, then mark the eye shapes with a felt tip pen before needling white wool into the shapes.

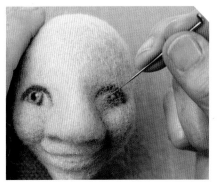

9 Using Merino wool for all the eye detailing, and dark brown for the upper eye lines, follow steps 4–6 on page 109, then needle a small dot of pink wool into the inner corner of each eye.

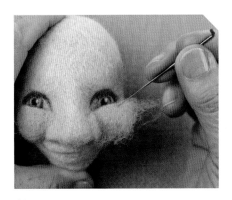

10 Needle felt two lower lids and attach them smoothly into the face.

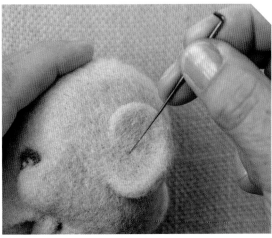

11 Needle felt the two ears. Splay out the fibres, press them onto the head and needle them into the head to secure. Needle into the centre of each ear to flatten them against the head.

Arms and legs

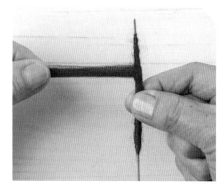

1 Arms First glue then wrap one arm wire up and down with thin lengths of red Merino wool until it is approximately 7mm (¼in) thick. Leave uncovered 1cm (½in) from one end and 2.5cm (1in) from the other end.

2 Glue one end of a thin length of black Merino wool to the arm and spiral it down to create a striped effect. Secure with glue. Repeat on the other arm.

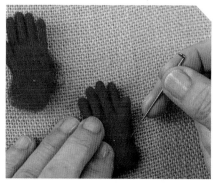

3 Gloved hands Needle felt two red gloves (see steps 14–16 on page 144).

4 Make a hole in the glove, glue the 1cm (½in) wire end and push it into the hole. Use a 38 triangle needle to work the loose fibres of the glove into the arm.

5 To edge the gloves wrap the wrists loosely with black coarse wool and needle lightly so that they remain fluffy.

6 Legs Bend the leg wire as shown in the diagram on page 175 and wrap with red and then black wools as described for the arms in steps 1 and 2 above.

7 Needle felt two boots using the template to help you with size and shape. Make a slit down each boot with a craft knife. Glue the feet wires and push one into each slit. Cover the slits with more wool and needle to smooth with the 38 triangle needle.

8 Needle felt two boot collars (see making a flat strip on page 42). Steam iron them to flatten, leaving the loose fibres, and neaten.

9 Wrap one round each ankle and needle the loose fibres into each boot to smooth the joins. Sew the laces onto each boot (see diagram on page 92).

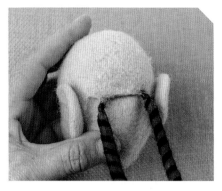

10 Cut a deep slit across the back of the head with the craft knife, glue the centre portion of the leg wire and push the wire firmly into the hole.

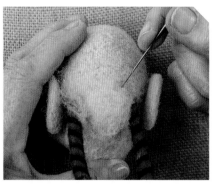

11 Use small amounts of wool and the 38 triangle needle to cover the hole and needle until really firm and secure, adding more wool if necessary.

12 Make a hole in the centre of each ear. Glue and insert the arms then needle a little flesh-coloured wool around the wires to secure.

Hair and hat

1 Using Herdwick wool, follow steps 1–4 on pages 135 and 136 to layer the hair.

2 Layer the strands sideways on one side to create the parting.

3 When complete give your doll a haircut and ruffle the layers slightly to give a wild and woolly look.

4 Needle in a little more Herdwick for the eyebrows. Fold small lengths for the moustache and the beard. Needle them into the face so that the fibres run downwards.

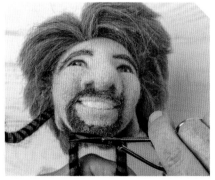

5 Trim and tidy up the moustache and beard using the curved embroidery scissors.

6 To make the hat, follow the instructions on pages 41 and 42 for the cylinder and flat circle. Use 4g (⅛oz) of wool for the cylinder (top) and the circle (brim). To finish, wrap a length of black Merino wool around the hat and needle to secure. Glue, then pin the hat to the head.

Book

1 Lay 4.5g (⅙oz) of wool on the pad and use the tip of the 40 triangle needle to pull the wool into a 14 x 9cm (5½ x 3½in) rectangle.

2 Needle the rectangle evenly, flipping it every now and again until it begins to firm up. Speed up the felting with the five-needle tool and also by rubbing it between your hands every now and again.

3 Finish with the twisted needle to smooth. Neaten the edge (see Tip on page 42), then steam iron the rectangle.

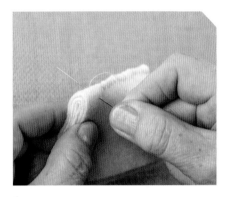

4 Layer three pieces of ready-made cream felt and fold them down the middle to create the pages. Oversew the folded edges to create the spine.

5 Trim the pages and neaten. Place the pages inside the cover, then glue the first and last pages to the inside of the cover.

6 Sew down the spine using brown cotton. Glue a 4cm (1½in) square of red felt to the front cover and embellish it with a black felt tip pen.

Finishing touches

1 Dust the cheeks and lips with a little red pastel powder. Spray lightly with fixative.

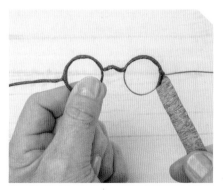

2 Glasses Bend the 45cm (17¾in) wire into the glasses shape (see template on page 175). Trim any excess wire. Wrap them tightly with waxed floral tape.

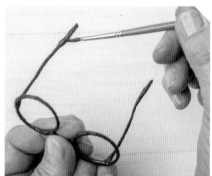

3 Bend the arms then paint the glasses red and place them on the nose. Secure with a spot of glue.

Sally Strangelove adores being centre stage with her jewelled glasses and curly Wensleydale locks. Her hat and boots are embellished with black net and we have given her a complete makeover with eyebrows to complement her hair and eyes, pastel pink rosy cheeks and happy smile.

Templates

The templates are all reproduced at actual size. The dotted lines represent the core size and the outer lines are the finished size. The wavy lines on the outlines indicate where loose fibres should be left so that one shape can be attached to another.

These templates are also available to download from the Bookmarked Hub: www.bookmarkedhub.com. Search for this book by title or ISBN: the files can be found under 'Book Extras'.

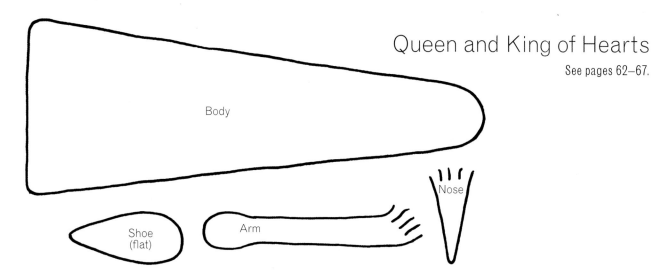

Queen and King of Hearts

See pages 62–67.

Body

Nose

Shoe (flat)

Arm

Danny Doodoll

See pages 68–75.

Body

Inner body core

Beige

Blue

Grey

Arm

Leg

Bag flap (flat)

Daisy's bag

Strap (flat)

Bag

Ear (flat)

Thumb

Daisy's bag flap (flat)

Little Dancer

See pages 76–83.

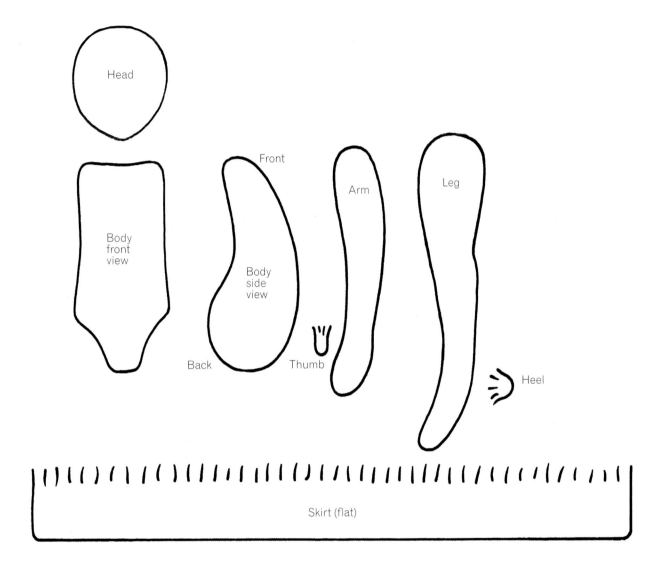

Head

Body front view

Front

Body side view

Back

Thumb

Arm

Leg

Heel

Skirt (flat)

Knitting Nigel

See pages 84–97.

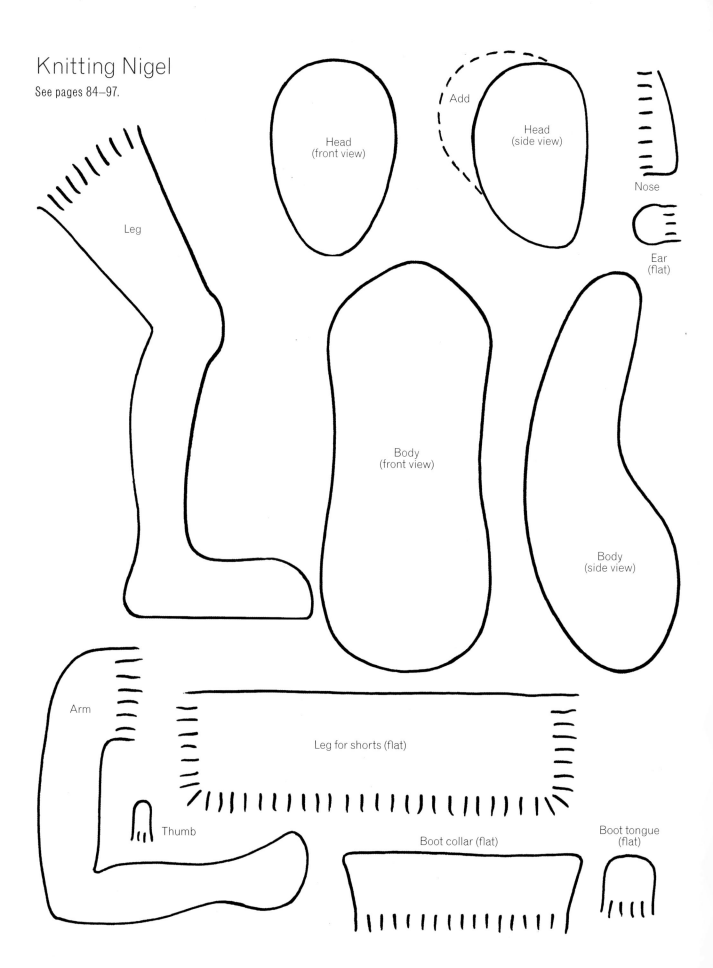

Leg

Head
(front view)

Add

Head
(side view)

Nose

Ear
(flat)

Body
(front view)

Body
(side view)

Arm

Leg for shorts (flat)

Thumb

Boot collar (flat)

Boot tongue
(flat)

Christmas Fairy

See pages 98–105.

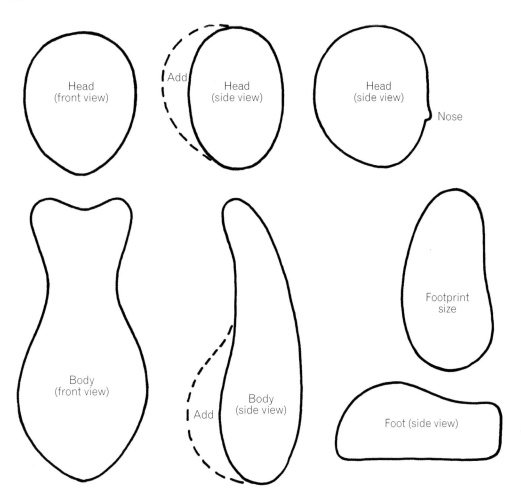

Wings

To complete the wings: wrap the trailing ends over the join, then twist them together.

Kawaii Kate

See pages 106–117.

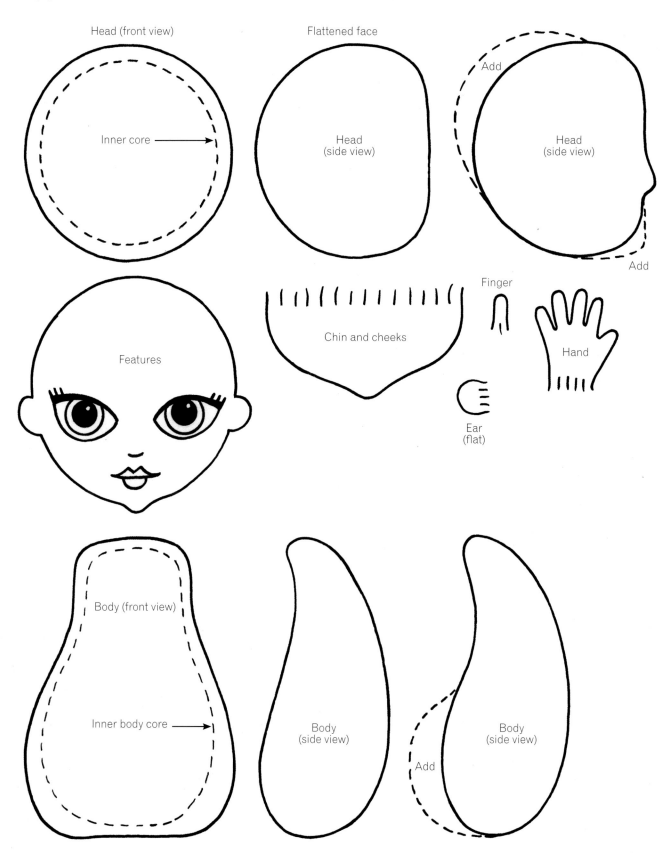

Head (front view)

Inner core

Flattened face

Head
(side view)

Add

Head
(side view)

Add

Features

Chin and cheeks

Finger

Hand

Ear
(flat)

Body (front view)

Inner body core

Body
(side view)

Add

Body
(side view)

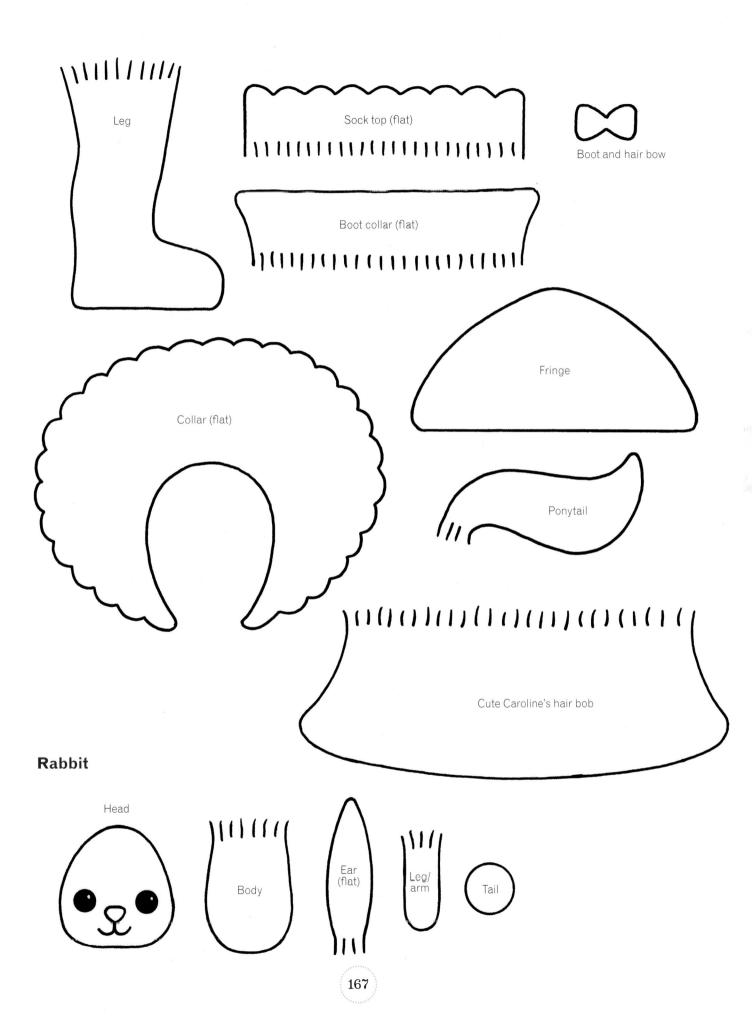

Leg

Sock top (flat)

Boot and hair bow

Boot collar (flat)

Collar (flat)

Fringe

Ponytail

Cute Caroline's hair bob

Rabbit

Head

Body

Ear (flat)

Leg/ arm

Tail

Silver Surfer

See pages 118–127.

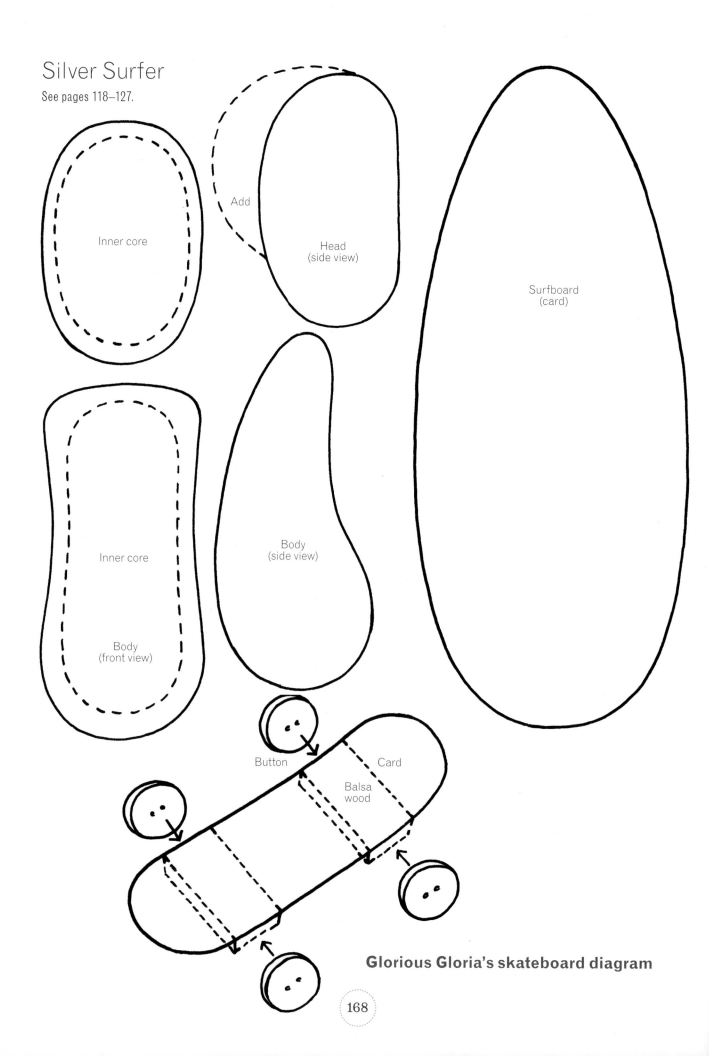

Inner core

Add

Head
(side view)

Surfboard
(card)

Inner core

Body
(side view)

Body
(front view)

Button

Card

Balsa
wood

Glorious Gloria's skateboard diagram

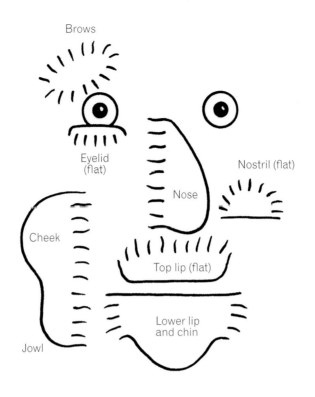

Brows

Eyelid (flat)

Nostril (flat)

Nose

Cheek

Top lip (flat)

Lower lip and chin

Jowl

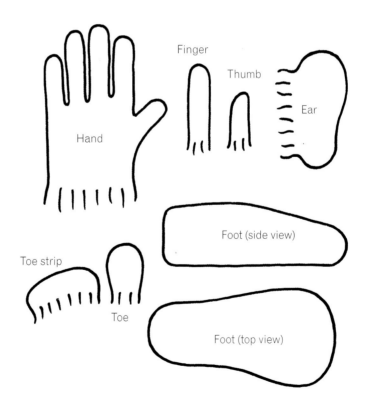

Finger

Thumb

Ear

Hand

Foot (side view)

Toe strip

Toe

Foot (top view)

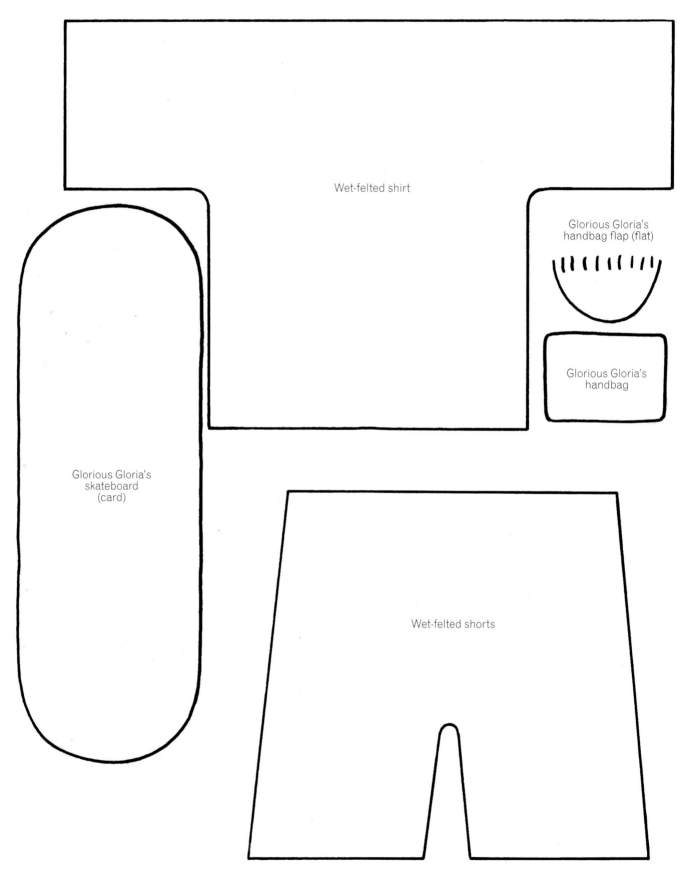

Wet-felted shirt

Glorious Gloria's
handbag flap (flat)

Glorious Gloria's
handbag

Glorious Gloria's
skateboard
(card)

Wet-felted shorts

Perfect Portraits

See pages 128–137.

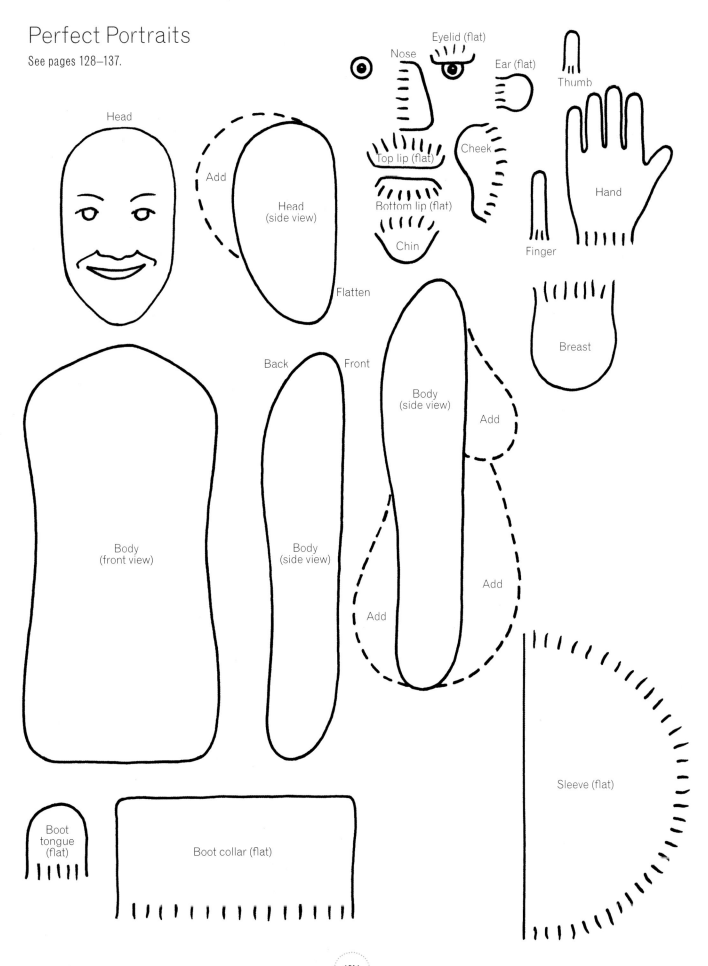

Head

Add

Head (side view)

Flatten

Nose

Eyelid (flat)

Ear (flat)

Thumb

Top lip (flat)

Cheek

Hand

Bottom lip (flat)

Chin

Finger

Breast

Back

Front

Body (side view)

Add

Body (front view)

Body (side view)

Add

Add

Add

Sleeve (flat)

Boot tongue (flat)

Boot collar (flat)

Perfect Portraits *continued*

See pages 128–137.

Sheep

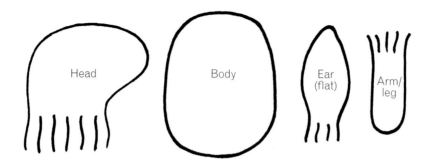

Mother Earth

See pages 138–153.

Map of the world

Mother Earth

See pages 138–153.

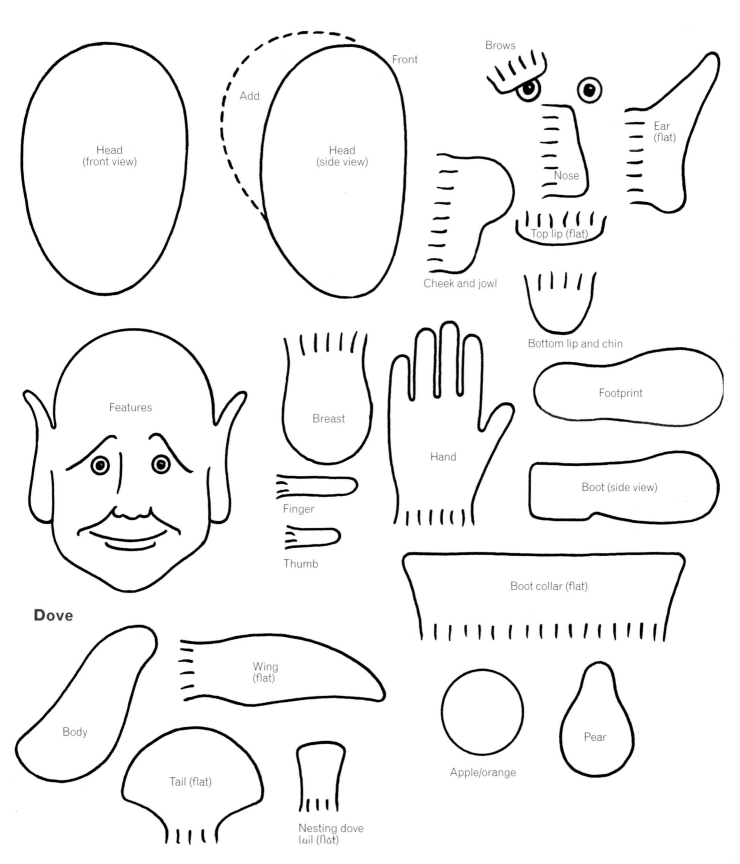

Head (front view)

Add

Head (side view)

Front

Brows

Nose

Ear (flat)

Top lip (flat)

Bottom lip and chin

Cheek and jowl

Features

Breast

Hand

Footprint

Finger

Thumb

Boot (side view)

Boot collar (flat)

Dove

Wing (flat)

Body

Tail (flat)

Nesting dove tail (flat)

Apple/orange

Pear

Weird and Wonderful

See pages 154–161.

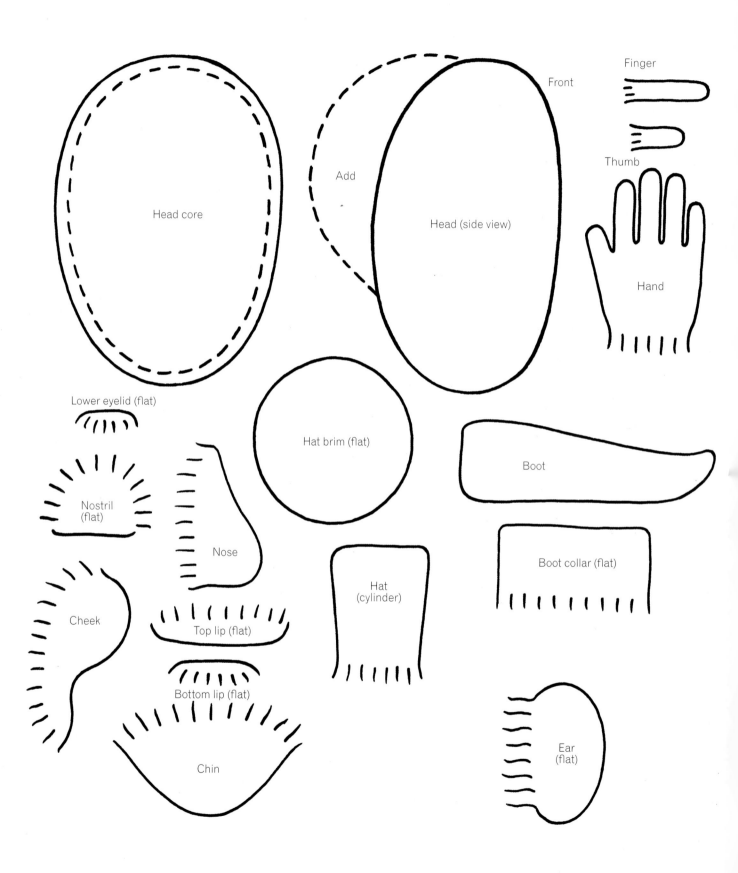

Head core

Add

Head (side view)

Front

Finger

Thumb

Hand

Lower eyelid (flat)

Hat brim (flat)

Boot

Nostril (flat)

Nose

Cheek

Top lip (flat)

Hat (cylinder)

Boot collar (flat)

Bottom lip (flat)

Chin

Ear (flat)

Glasses

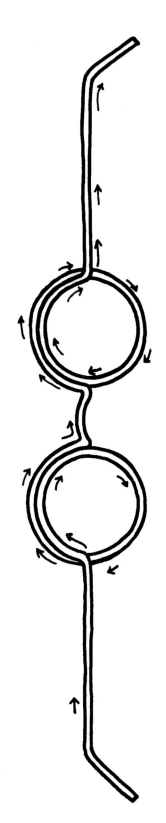

Legs

Bend and wrap the wire as shown
to create the legs and feet.

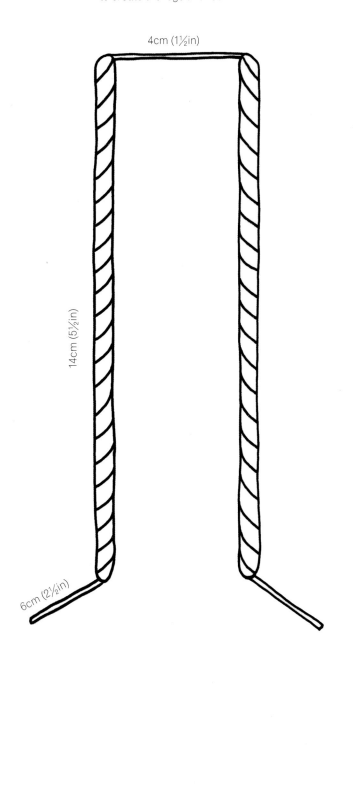

4cm (1½in)

14cm (5½in)

6cm (2½in)

Index